I0817482

...elcome to ...working

...TYLISH PROJECTS
...R HOME & GARDEN

MOA BRÄNNSTRÖM OTT

Originally published as *Trä* by Natur & Kultur, Stockholm, Sweden, ©2017
Translated from the Swedish by Carol Huebscher Rhoades

Library of Congress Control Number: 2024941473

Cover design by Lori Ehrlich
Type set in Lagstrom Grotesk / Janson Hemlos

ISBN: 978-0-7643-6922-3
Printed in India

Published by Schiffer Publishing, Ltd.
4880 Lower Valley Road
Atglen, PA 19310
Phone: (610) 593-1777; Fax: (610) 593-2002
Email: Info@schifferbooks.com
Web: www.schifferbooks.com

For our complete selection of fine books on this and related subjects, please visit our website at www.schifferbooks.com. You may also write for a free catalog.

Schiffer Publishing's titles are available at special discounts for bulk purchases for sales promotions or premiums. Special editions, including personalized covers, corporate imprints, and excerpts, can be created in large quantities for special needs. For more information, contact the publisher.

We are always looking for people to write books on new and related subjects.
If you have an idea for a book, please contact us at proposals@schifferbooks.com.

A FEELING FOR WOOD

I HAVE AN ENORMOUS RESPECT FOR WOOD as a material. That a tree grew a whole lifetime before it became a plank to which I'll take a saw has earned my consideration and respect. When working with wood, it's important to recognize its characteristics and limitations. It's a living material, and I think that one should handle wood with that in mind.

I trained as a furniture maker at Capellagården on the Swedish island of Öland, at Carl Malmsten's handcraft school. However, my interest in cabinet making began a long time earlier. At *gymnasium* (senior high school), I took a handcraft course with emphasis on fine carpentry, and even as a child, I collected sticks and loved sitting and carving on the kitchen floor. In short, you could say that wood has been a lifelong passion.

The most common reaction I get when I tell people that I work as a cabinetmaker is "Ah, how cool it must be; I would love to do woodworking." And my answer is always "So, do it." However, most people don't know how or where to begin. Where do you buy materials, and which wood is good for what, what tools are needed, and how do you use them?

When I was asked about writing a carpentry handbook, I didn't give it a second thought. Of course I would do it. I responded exactly as everyone who said, "Ah, how cool!"—it was time to get going with my own carpentry dreams. You don't have to be a man and have a whole machine shop at home to be able to do woodwork. All you need is a rather well-filled toolbox, accuracy, and patience to be able to make really nice things.

I was born and grew up in Stockholm, but my family comes from Västerbotten (a county in northern Sweden). We have a family home in Västerbotten's interior, which I visit as often as possible. I find quiet there, and I usually say that I have a northerner's soul. I believe that when I'm in the city, I can experience a little of that quiet and security through my daily contact with wood, despite the city's hectic pace. It has become a link between me and the forest.

As a cabinetmaker, my extreme accuracy is both my best and worst characteristic. When I'm working on a project, there is a constant compromise between time and finessing. Therefore, it's most fun to make things for myself. That way, there is nothing to determine how long it should take. I can decide for myself what it should look like, and make the measurements and sizing precisely as I want. I assume that this is what most are out after when they want to do woodworking for their own home. And, of course, to enjoy the feeling of "I made this myself; I'm so awesome!"

/Moa

Pine
Birch
Oak
Spruce
Beech
Ash
Witch elm
Larch
Maple
Linden
Aspen
Alder

THE FOREST AND WOOD

Wood is a fantastic material. It's a multifaceted natural product offering a multitude of possibilities. It is, in relation to its weight, a strong, stable, and durable material. In addition, it's such an important part of ecology, which makes it particularly special. For me, it's important to remember that every bit of wood was actually a part of a tree. Wood is not just piles of boards at a lumberyard. The planks I set my saw to have probably been on the earth longer than I have. The tree stood in its forest and grew large and powerful to end up as a board that I can make into something. For me, this includes the responsibility to do something good with it and to handle it with care and respect. Even after a tree has been felled and cut into lumber, it continues to be a living material, affected by the surrounding environment. It reacts to heat and humidity, and to a certain extent, it always moves in step with the seasons. In the spring, when it's damp, it swells, and in winter when it's drier, the wood shrinks.

Trees are amazing organisms. Besides the role they play in the ecological system as a whole, trees interact with each other and are well-planned to the smallest detail. There are about 50,000 species of trees worldwide, and some can be several thousands of years old.

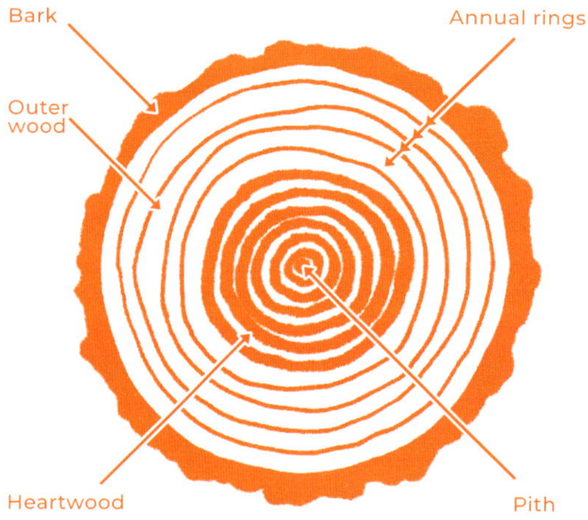

If you look at a crosscut of a tree trunk, you can see that is built up of various layers.

The outermost layer is the outer bark, which protects the inner layers against, for example, hard weather and diseases. In the tree's crown, where the leaves are, the process called photosynthesis takes energy from the sunlight and sends nutrition down through the inner bark to the rest of the tree. Just inside the inner bark is the cambium layer, a thin layer that is the basis of the tree's growth in diameter. It's also here that the new annual rings are created. An annual ring is, exactly as the name implies, the amount of growth the tree makes in one year.

Wood is unbelievably strong when aligned with the direction of its fibers, but weaker between the annual rings. Depending on how quickly the tree grows, the distance between the rings can vary. A tree that grows slowly will have more closely spaced rings and will thus be stronger. The annual growth is divided into spring wood and summer wood. In the spring, when the frost melts on the ground and the water almost floods up into the tree, the spring wood is lighter. It has larger pores and therefore becomes softer. After that, the summer wood is darker and stronger wood that forms during the more nutrition-poor growth period. On some trees—pine, for example—the annual rings are obvious. On others, such as birch, they are almost indistinguishable. By looking at the crosscut of a tree, you have insight into each year of its life. Among other things, you can see if it has been damaged, if it had some disease, and which summers were dry.

The wood closest to the bark is called sapwood or surface wood, and it has the youngest annual rings. They are often lighter and have the purpose of transporting minerals from the roots to the leaves. Inside the sapwood is the heartwood. It's the oldest wood and it contains the nutrition, oils, and resin, which make it darker and harder than sapwood. Heartwood doesn't contain as much water as sapwood and is, therefore, more stable. Heartwood

is the best wood for carpentry. The heartwood continues all the way in to the pith, the center of the tree.

Softwood and Hardwood Species

Trees are divided into two groups: hard and soft wood species. The terms "hardwood" and "softwood" are botanical designations that really don't say much about the tree's physical strength. However, hardwood trees usually grow more slowly than the softwoods and thus usually have harder wood, but that does not apply to all species.

Softwoods are mainly from conifers, trees with "naked" seeds. Fir, spruce, larch, cedar, and redwood are examples of softwood species that are used for furniture making. They show a clear difference between spring and summer wood: spring wood is lighter and soft, while summer wood is darker and hard, creating more obvious annual rings in the tree.

There are more hardwood species, and they come from different leafy trees with "covered" seeds. The most common ones used for carpentry are birch, beech, alder, oak, ash, elm, maple, linen, walnut, cherry, teak, and mahogany. The hardwood trees have a more complex cell structure than the softwood species, and the color and look can be very different among these trees. Some have large pores and others quite small pores, which influences the look, hardness, texture, and overall characteristics.

At the Lumberyard

When you visit the lumberyard to choose wood, there are a few things to think about so you'll go home with the best possible material. Never be afraid to ask for help if you feel unsure—the clerks are there to help you!

Pine is a good wood to begin with because it's easy to work with and inexpensive, which means that you'll have the means for a do-over in case something goes wrong. Once you're a little more familiar with woods, it'll be fun to test birch, oak, and ash. In general, however, I think you should choose a wood species that you think is fine and that has the qualities most suitable for your project.

Hardwood

Trees are always sawed up into lengths, and the side that is perpendicular to the direction of the wood fiber (the grain) is called the end wood. The tree is sawed in various dimensions and designated outside at the lumberyard, such as wood, planks, lumber, decking, and battens or strips, depending on what they are used for.

There are three types of lumber: A, B, and C. A is the highest quality, with few or no knots, more heartwood, and most often rather densely grown. It's used for finer woodwork and is also the type you should look out for. Type A has subcategories, A1–A4, with A1 the finest. Type B is used for building and type C, for example, is for packaging.

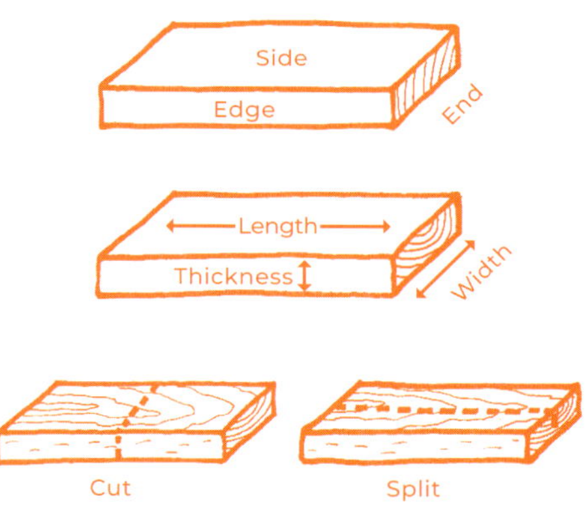

When choosing your wood, you should make sure that the boards don't have any unwanted knots or splits. The number of knots is, for the most part, an aesthetic factor, but splits are to be avoided for the sake of durability. A split might be larger than you see with your eyes, and it can split even more when you store the board at room temperature. Also make sure that the boards are relatively straight on all sides. If you're going to saw it up into short lengths, you can be more forgiving, but if you want longer pieces, they should be as straight as possible. For best durability and stability of the boards, you should make sure that the end wood is approximately at a 45° angle.

You should also choose boards with tight annual rings and a lot of

End wood with annual rings at 45° angle

heartwood because it's the strongest and most stable.

At the lumberyard, boards are most often stored in a large outer room at a slightly lower temperature and higher humidity (about 20 percent) than the inside area. The most desirable humidity level for fine woodworking is about 6 percent. When you take your boards home and store them inside, they will dry out rather quickly, so there is a great risk that the wood will deteriorate. In order for the wood to deteriorate as little as possible, you must make sure that the air can move freely around all the boards. You can do this by laying all the boards on battens (thin wood rails), instead of laying them directly on the floor.

If you have many boards and need to pile them, you can place a batten between every board. This way, the air can circulate, and the boards can dry evenly.

Sheets of Wood

Sheets are made of wood fiber such as chipboard or MDF (medium-density fiberboard, a wood composite engineered from leftover hardwood or softwood). There is not much difference in look and quality between various sheets of the same type. The only thing you need to think about when choosing sheets is that they aren't damaged on the edges or have unwanted markings. When choosing plywood sheets, there are a few things to be concerned about. Because they are made in thin layers of solid wood, they can, in some instances, be crooked, and it can be difficult to straighten crooked plywood, especially when it gets a little thicker.

Also check any veins and knots when choosing plywood and glued wood sheets. Choose a sheet that has a pattern in the veins that you like, because the look can vary rather a lot from sheet to sheet. I always think that it's worth checking through a batch to find the finest pieces.

TOOLS AND TECHNIQUES

Before you begin woodworking, it's a good idea to become familiar with the tools that are suitable to have at home and to learn how to use them. In this chapter, I will go through a number of joining techniques that I often use myself. These techniques are used for the projects in the book and are a good basis for your future woodworking.

Woodworking at Home

You don't need a garage full of machines to produce well-made, fine furniture. You don't even need to have a carpenter's bench, because you can just as easily use a kitchen table for your work surface. Just lay out a flat sheet of wood such as builder's plywood that you don't need to be afraid of damaging. Buy cut wood at the lumberyard in the size you think suitable, perhaps around 39⅜ × 47¼ in. (1,000 x 1,200 mm). Take out the sheet when you're going to work with it and store it when you're finished. You can even buy collapsible work benches with cranks and holes for clamps. For my part, I think it's nice to have a classic woodworker's bench at home, although I live in an apartment. It's practical not only when you want to make something, but also because it's a stylish and engaging piece. It makes it feel more normal to take out a piece of wood and begin to carve or do woodworking.

In this chapter, you'll find information about the most important tools you'll need. There are an awful lot of different types of specialized tools for various purposes, at quite a few different price points. So, I suggest that you begin by simply making a basic list. It doesn't have to be for the most expensive types—buy at a medium price range, look for the tools you need most, and, if you want, you can upgrade later on to even better tools.

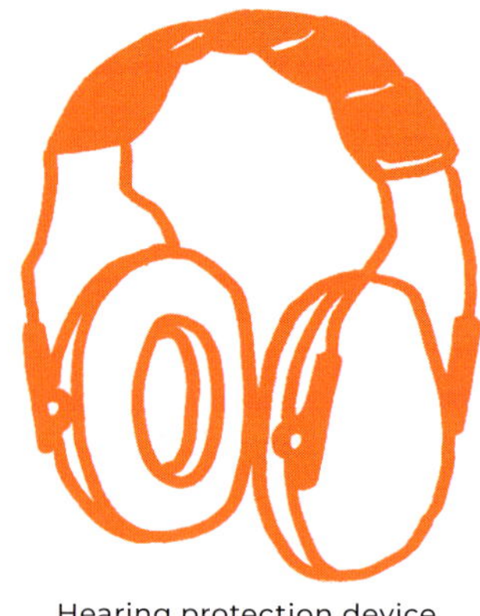
Hearing protection device

First-aid kit

Face mask

Handling Your Tools and Safety

To avoid injuries, you must handle your tools safely and sensibly. Make sure that your work tool is secured when you chisel, bore, and saw. If you have long hair, tie it in a knot when you bore or screw, so it won't get caught in any electric tool. Always be aware of where your fingers, hands, and body are, so they are not in the way of any tool as you work in case you slip. Always try to cut away from yourself when you work with sharp edges.

Accidents can happen even if you're careful. It's easy to slip a little with a chisel or scratch yourself with a saw. Usually, you won't suffer any serious injuries, but, for safety's sake, it's important to have a first-aid kit nearby. You can buy boxes or small bags with all the basics. Make sure that your kit's always complete—if you use something, replace it right away so it won't be missing when you need it next time.

If you're working with noisy electric tools, you must use hearing protection like earmuffs or earplugs. Even when you're hammering or hitting with a mallet, it's good to have protection for your ears. If you're grinding without an extractor or vacuum, you should wear a face mask because wood dust can create irritations in your airways.

MEASURING

Measuring and marking correctly are important aspects of woodwork. If you're not precise with measuring and measurements, you'll pay later on in the project. So, take it easy and make sure that the measurements and angles are as exact as possible. The expression "Measure twice and cut once" is perhaps a little clichéd, but the feeling you'll get when you've measured sloppily makes the adage worth repeating. Measuring is easier with good tools, the most important of which you'll find below. (Measurements in this book are given in both inches/feet and millimeters/meters, with millimeters from the original Swedish text and inches rounded to the closest equivalent.)

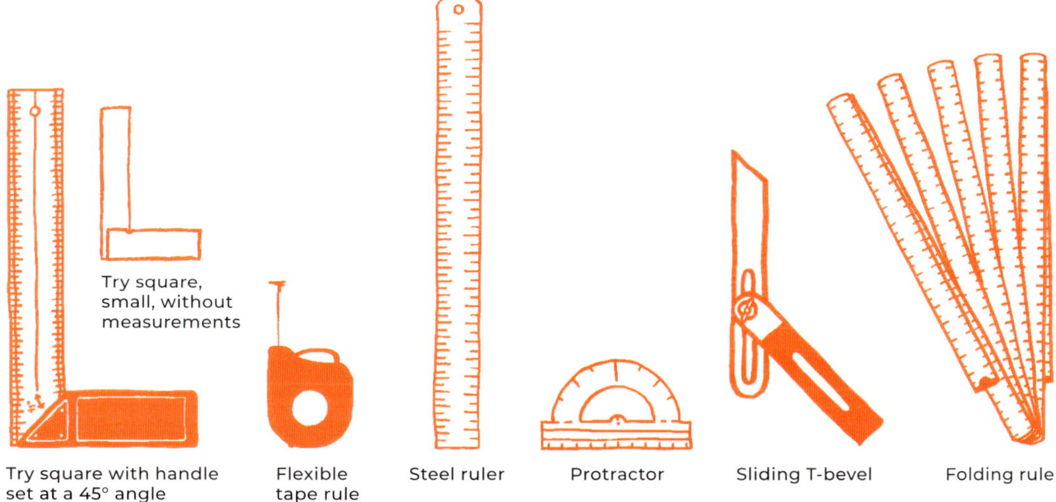

Folding Rule

There are several different types of folding rule; most are 6½–8 feet (2–2.4 meters) long, measured in inches (centimeters and millimeters). I recommend choosing a good-quality one so you can depend on the accuracy of the measurements and joints that move smoothly. Some folding rules only indicate inches on one side, and centimeters on the other. The correct name is a meter rule, but because folding rule is such an established name, I use it, nevertheless.

My personal favorite is a Hultafors contact-meter, which is constructed for easier measuring directly against an underlying support. As far as its measuring function is concerned, it doesn't matter if your folding rule is plastic or wood, but of course, I prefer the feeling of wood.

Measuring Tape and Flexible Tape Rule

In principle, measuring tapes and flexible tape rules have the same function as a folding rule, but they are more flexible and are available in longer lengths than a folding rule. The measuring band on a flexible tape rule is made of steel and is stiffer than a measuring tape, which means it functions well for both internal and external measurements, circumference and diameter. The band catches at the length you draw it out to and slides in at the press of a button.

A little spike, which can be used to punch a mark directly onto the wood, sits at the far end of a flexible tape rule. The black scale shows the measurement from the tape rule's opening, and the red scale shows the measurement from a tongue on the back of the rule. The red scale is used primarily for internal measurements.

I prefer a flexible tape rule to a measuring tape and recommend that you buy a good-quality one. The longer-length ones, 16–26 feet (5–8 meters), are intended for coarser measurements, so the end catch is usually not accurate enough to be a depended on when you're working in millimeters. A Talmeter (flexible tape rule) is actually a brand name for a specific product, the product type called a marking measure tape.

Ruler

When you're measuring or marking shorter pieces, it's easier to use a ruler instead of a folding rule or measuring tape because a ruler is so easy to handle. Use a ruler intended for woodworking, with measurements in centimeters and millimeters. A metal ruler with inset markings with measurements beginning at one end is the most useful. They are the most precise, which is necessary when you're measuring millimeters.

Always lean over the ruler so you can look down straight from above and be assured that you're drawing precisely in line with the ruler's markings.

Try Square

A try square is used for drawing a right-angle line or for controlling right angles. There are many sizes and varieties of try squares available. I think it's a good idea to have two different models: one with a measuring scale of about 6–8 inch (150–200 mm), where the top short side of the piece shows a 45° angle, and one with a smaller blade of about 2–4 inch (50–100 mm).

Use a try square when you draw markings to follow for a straight line. You'll see how to on the next page.

To make sure that a cut is precisely 90°, lay the handle against the side so the blade is placed over the cut you want to check. Hold the wood piece and try square against a light source so you can see if the cut is at a right angle. If light shows between the piece of wood and the blade on the try square, the angle is not exact.

Sliding T Bevel and Protractor

A sliding T bevel is an adjustable tool that can be used to lock in various angles. You'll use it when you need to draw a particular angle on a workpiece or to transfer an angle from one piece to another. You won't see the angle set on the sliding T bevel itself. To read the angle you have or want to set in, you'll need a protractor.

Drawing Straight with a Try Square

The try square makes straight lines with the correct angle. Use a sharpened pencil.

Hook the handle against the side of the piece of wood. Make sure that the blade lies where you want to draw a straight line.

Hold the handle steady against the piece and make sure that the blade lies flat. Then, draw a line along the blade with a pencil.

Using a Sliding T Bevel

1. Set the T bevel to the angle you want, with the help of a protractor. Set the handle of the T bevel close to the underside of the straight part of the protractor and adjust the blade until it lands at the angle you want. The blade should always go from the center of the protractor to your chosen angle.

Lock the T bevel when you have set it at the angle you want, with the locking screw either at the side or end of the sliding T bevel.

2. Lay the T bevel against the piece of wood, precisely as you do with a try square, with the handle firmly against the side and the blade flat on the wood surface. Draw the line along the blade.

SAWS

You'll saw a lot when you do woodworking, so it'll be easier to use saws that are particularly made for cabinetry. There's the old honorable backsaw in all its glory, but it's not so good when it's important to make a fine saw cut. A better choice is a saw with a thinner blade and smaller teeth. There are various types of saws suitable for fine woodwork, and my recommendation is for the Japanese varieties.

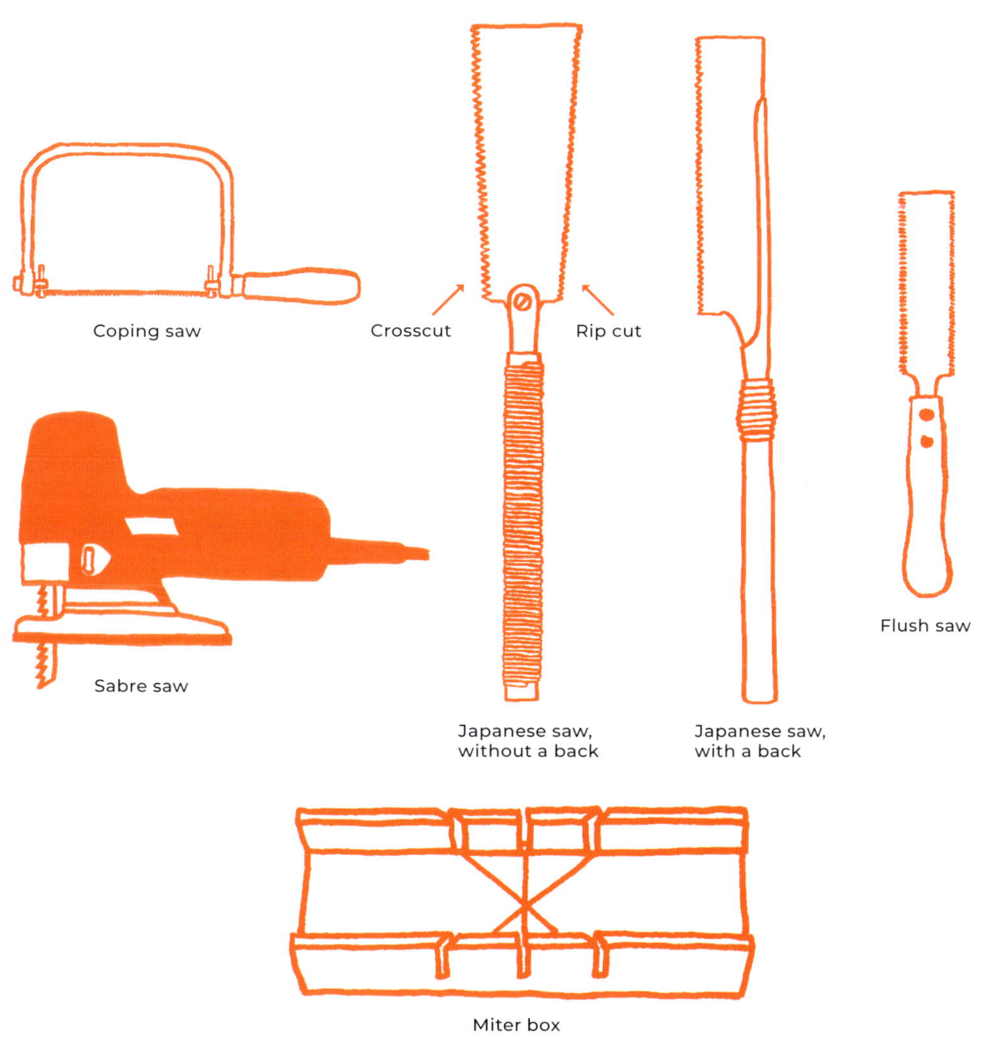

Japanese Saw

Japanese saws, or pull saws (as they are also called), cut material when you pull the saw toward you instead of when pushing it away. They can therefore have a thin, fine blade and fine sawteeth, and they don't bend as you pull. You can find models with various sizes of teeth and different blade lengths as well as with or without a back. I recommend that you buy two Japanese saws: one somewhat larger model with a back and an approximately 9½ inch (240 mm) long blade. It should have very fine teeth and will make delicate cuts but is more versatile than a smaller variant because you can saw a deeper cut. The back helps hold the blade stiff, and you can therefore make a straighter cut.

A good complement is a Japanese saw without a back, but instead, with a crosscut side and a rip-cut side. That means that the teeth on one side are to crosscut, and the teeth on the other side are to rip cut; in other words, straight across the grain or, alternatively, along the grain. The blade on these saws is usually a little thicker than on those with a back (now we're talking of tenths of millimeters) to hold it stiff without a back. Work cautiously with your Japanese saws, because the teeth are so fine that they can easily break. Do not saw in any material other than wood, and follow the saw's cutting speed. Most Japanese saws have interchangeable blades.

Flush Saw

A flush saw is a fine-tooth pulling saw with a thin flexible blade about 6 inches (150 mm) long, often with teeth on both sides. The saw is good for sawing pegs, dowels, and the like, when you want to place the saw cut as close to the wood surface as possible. The flush saw has no set on its teeth, which means that the width of the teeth is the same as the width of the blade. Regular saws have teeth set slightly outward alternately to left and right, to cut more material than the width of the saw blade, so the wood doesn't catch in the sawblade when you're sawing.

Coping Saw

A coping saw is used, for example, to cut curves and irregular shapes. It has a fine, narrow blade, which makes it easy to move in different directions. The blade can also be set crosswise in relation to the back, which you'll need to do if the piece being worked on is wider than the depth of the bow. The angle of the blade can be changed by twisting the handle to loosen the tension on the blade. So, you turn the two pegs at the respective ends of the saw blade in the desired direction and then tension the handle again.

Sabre Saw

A sabre saw is an electric handheld saw with a small saw blade between approximately 2½ and 4 inches (60 and 105 mm) long, which moves up and down quickly as you saw. There are various blades for different materials, so make sure you choose the blade for wood. Of all the various electric handsaws available, I think that the sabre saw is easiest to use and the least dangerous. It's a versatile saw that can cut both straight lines and curves. You can easily cut a hole in a sheet of wood by first boring a hole where the sabre saw blade will go, then sawing out the shape you want at the hole. A sabre saw functions best for cutting sheet material and thinner boards. Always make sure to have a sharp and straight sawblade; otherwise, the cut will be a little crooked and the wood will chip.

Always make sure your piece of wood is properly secured, with the line you want to cut free and outside the work surface. Hold the saw steady against the wood and make sure that the saw comes up in one movement before you begin to saw; otherwise, the blade can stick in the piece of wood and make the saw skip. The blade saws upward, so the wood can chip on the top as you saw. One tip for achieving a fine front is to draw the markings for what it'll be on the back and then have that side turned upward for sawing.

Miter Box

A miter box is a wooden or plastic box with slots to guide cutting for 45° and 90° angles. Some boxes have more angles, but these two are what are used most. Use the box together with a Japanese saw or another fine saw so you can cut precise angles. Choose a box with relatively narrow slots for more exact cutting.

Cutting with a Coping Saw

Secure the piece on the work surface so that the line you want to saw is free and outside the work surface.

Sit down so you have the piece at approximately chest height in front of you. That way, you can more easily see that you're cutting at the right angle. When you cut, the sawblade should be vertical. Do not press down too much or the sawblade will catch—follow the saw as it cuts the wood.

If you're going to make a sharp turn, saw at the same place several times at the same time as you turn the blade in the direction you'll continue the saw cut. This way, you'll cut a small space for the sawblade to move in.

When you cut so far into the piece that the back of the saw is at the edge of the wood, you can turn the sawblade so the back ends up on the side instead of straight behind. This will work out better. It might happen that the waste wood side catches in the back although you turned the blade. You can coarsely saw away the pieces from the waste wood side with, for example, a Japanese saw—just enough so you have space inside the bow of the saw.

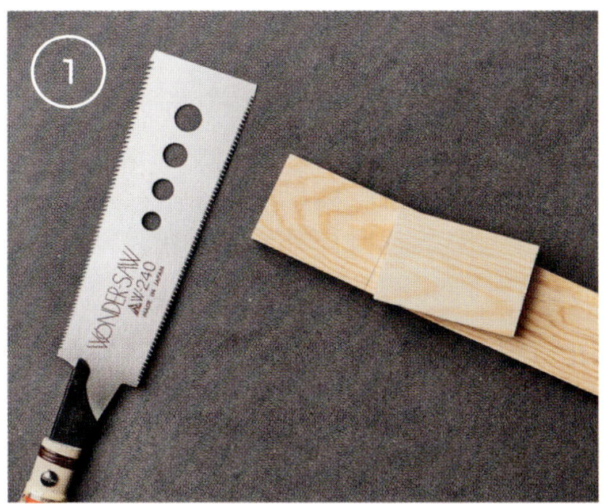

Sawing with a Block

1. Secure the wood piece on the work surface with a clamp so it'll stay steady as you saw. To make it easier to make a straight cut, you can hold or firmly secure a square block aligned with the line you want to saw, as a support for the sawblade.

2. Make sure that the sawblade runs along with the block; make a straight cut both downward and forward.

Sawing without a Block

If you're sawing with a Japanese saw without using a block or miter box, you can keep track of the wood piece as it's mirrored in the sawblade. If the mirroring is completely in line with the piece of wood, it means that you're holding the saw at a 90° angle. If, at the same time as you're cutting, you see throughout that the mirror image is straight, the cut will also be straight.

Miter

1. Use the handle on the try square with a 45° angle or set a sliding T bevel at a 45° angle and draw the angle at the desired place on your piece. If possible, set the markings so there is material left on both sides of the line. This will make the sawing much easier.

2. Put the piece in the miter box and use a Japanese saw to cut in the slot for a 45° angle. This'll be easier if you secure the piece in the box with a clamp.

3. Saw all the ends and test to ensure that, when together, they make a 90° angle at each corner without gaps. Adjust the angles with a file if they gap, but make sure not to round off the cuts. It's important that the mitering be as tight as possible if it'll be glued together. The glued joint will not be strong if the ends don't touch each other all along the entire surface.

You can find out how to glue a miter on page 59.

PLANING

Planing is a very pleasant and satisfactory job, but it can be quite difficult for a beginner to do well at first. It takes a lot of practice with the handle and also knowledge about the plane, as well as how it should be cared for so that the results will be good. In this book, most projects use ready-planed wood, but of course, you might choose to do the planing yourself.

Wooden jack plane

Bench plane

Metal jack plane

Jack Plane

A jack plane is a medium-size plane with a sole about 8–11¾ inches (200–300 mm) long that is intended for "polishing" the finish on a wood piece before grinding. You can find both wooden and metal versions. I think this is a good all-around plane because it can plane flat surfaces and angles, but at the same time, it's handy enough for finishing touches.

Bench Plane

A bench plane is a smaller plane that you grasp with one hand. It has a little cutting angle for planing off end wood, but it also functions well for planing joints and edges. It's smooth and easy to handle thanks to its size, although for the same reason, it's not very good for planing flat surfaces.

Planing

Make sure that the plane steel is sharp and the plane is correctly installed.

If you don't have a plane bench stop, you can secure a stop block on the work surface at a 90° angle from the edge of the work surface. The stop block and clamp together must be more secure than the wood piece you'll plane. Place one end of the wood piece against the stop block and then plane toward the block.

Check to see how the grain goes in your workpiece. Place the wood piece so you always plane in the direction of the wood grain. Keep an even pressure throughout the planing and check often with the try square to ensure that the angle is right. If you plane against the grain, there is a great risk that the wood will splinter. You should quickly notice if you're planing in the wrong direction because the plane will catch in the wood and the plane won't move forward smoothly.

Planing Glued Joints

When planing a glued joint, you place the plane so you produce thin shavings. It can be difficult to see which direction the grain runs in the wood when you can't see the edges on the boards. Carefully test to find which direction it'll be easiest to plane in. If you hold the plane at an angle over the joint, the blade will cut more easily than if you hold it completely straight. If the grain direction in two joined pieces goes in different directions, depending on which direction you plane, to partially to cut in the grain direction—it's easier if you plane as little wood as possible on each pass of the plane.

CHISELS AND JOINING

Chiseling is a very pleasant and useful method of woodworking. If you don't have a lot of electric machines, you'll need to use your chisels a lot. If you've never used a chisel before, it's a good idea to practice on a waste piece before you go into your workpiece.

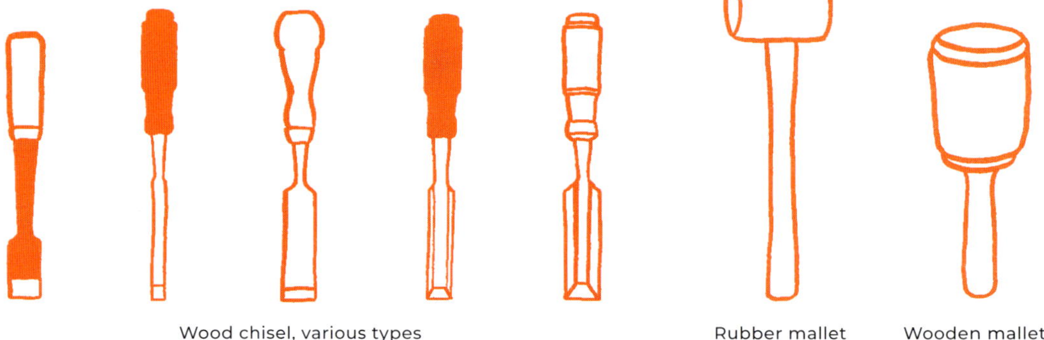

Wood chisel, various types

Rubber mallet

Wooden mallet

Wood Chisel

A wood chisel is cutting tool with a straight edge used for chipping away wood. The edge has a flat and a tapered side. Always have the flat side turned toward the wood that will remain, and the tapered side toward the waste wood.

Chisels come in many different sizes, and it's good to have a set-on iron blade between ¼ and 1¼ inches (6 and 30 mm). The shaft can be wood or plastic. It's worth buying a better-quality chisel because the sharpness of the steel will last longer. Always work with a sharp blade and be cautious of the edge. Always use a wooden mallet when hitting a chisel—a hammer can damage the shaft.

Wooden Mallet

A wooden mallet is a mallet with both the shaft and head of a hardwood such as birch or beech. The mallet is either lathed in one piece, or the shaft and head are two joined pieces. A wooden mallet is used for hitting a chisel to drive in dowel pins and to join joints.

Rubber Mallet

A rubber mallet has a wooden shaft and rubber head. These are good to use when you want to drive joints together because they don't leave any hit marks on the wood.

Lap Joint, Corner

1. Mark where you want your recess on both pieces. You can use the piece that will be fitted in and mark using the edge on it, so you'll have the mark at exactly the right width. Draw the line with the try square and a sharp pencil.

2. Continue drawing the line down on the sides to half the thickness of the board. Make the long side of the line out to the end wood and then on the other side, so all the waste wood is encircled. This line can be made with a marking gauge, but I think it's easiest to place the tip of the pencil at the desired place and lay one of your fingers to hold the pencil as a support on the underside of the wood, and then drag the pencil along the side.

Outline the waste wood so you can more easily see what is to be removed.

3. Cut at a 90° angle in the miter box with a Japanese saw, precisely at the waste wood side of your marking. Be careful that you don't saw more than you should, and make sure that you cut to the same depth on both sides.

4. Secure the piece onto the work surface with one or two clamps.

5. Chisel away the waste wood. Use a sharp chisel and a wooden mallet. Chisel away a little at a time, with the tapered side of the chisel against the waste wood and the flat side turned to the material that will remain. If the chisel is turned the wrong way, the cut won't be right angled and smooth.

6. To even out the surface and fit, you cut away the last material with a chisel by hand, or alternatively, a file. I personally prefer cutting with a chisel.

7. Also make sure that the saw cut on the neck is even and fine and that no material remains that should have been cut away at the corner on the neck.

8. Spread glue on the contact surfaces and clamp together. Place a small piece of wood, cork, or something similar between the wood and clamp so you don't leave press marks on the wood. Double check the right angle with a try square.

Lap Joint, Cross

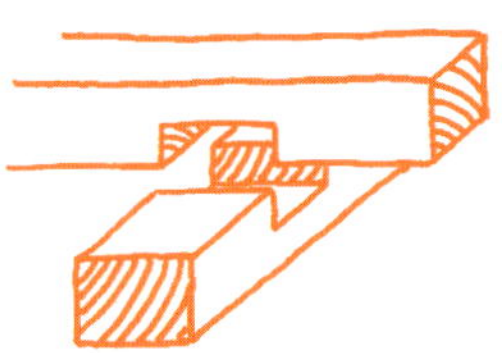

1. Mark where you want the recess on both pieces. You can use the piece that will fit in and mark the edges on it, so you'll make the mark at exactly the right width.

2. Draw the line with the try square and a sharp pencil. Continue the line down on the sides to half the thickness of the board and then make a lengthening line inside the markings, which show the depth of the recess. Outline the waste wood so you can more easily see what needs to be cut away.

3. Cut at a 90° angle in the miter box with a Japanese saw, precisely at the waste wood side of your marking. Be careful that you don't saw more than you should and make sure that you saw to the same depth on both sides.

4. Secure the piece onto the work surface with one or two clamps, either standing or lying, and chisel away the waste wood. Use a sharp chisel and wooden mallet. Chisel a little at a time, with the tapered side of the chisel turned against the waste wood, and then flat side against the material to remain. If the chisel is turned in the

wrong direction, the cut will not be at a right angle and smooth.

Chisel a little at a time. In order to even out the surface and fit it in, cut the last material away with a chisel by hand, or a file. Personally, I prefer cutting with a chisel.

5. Also make sure that the saw cut on the neck is even and fine and that no material remains that should have been cut away at the corners.

6. Spread glue on the contact surfaces and clamp together. Place a small piece of wood, cork, or something similar between the wood and clamp so you don't leave press marks on the wood. Double check the right angle with a try square.

Mortise-and-Tenon Joint

1. Mark the depth of the slot on the end of one piece of wood. Continue the line around the whole piece of wood, using a try square. Divide the end into three equal sections; the center section will be the tongue. Use your finger as a support precisely as you did for the lap joint. Outline the waste wood.

2. With the board in a miter box, use a Japanese saw to cut down to the tenon on both sides. Make sure you don't saw into the tenon.

3. Secure the piece of wood and chisel the waste wood away with a chisel and mallet. Match the width of the chisel to the width of the wood—the narrower the wood, the narrower the chisel, and the wider the wood, the wider the chisel. Break the surface (i.e., round the edges with a chisel, a file, or sandpaper). Make sure that the tongue is evenly thick and the slots are squared.

4. Measure the exact thickness of the tenon and transfer it to the other wood piece which will have the slot. Also, mark the depth of the slot and outline the waste wood.

5. Secure the wood piece to the workbench so the slot end is free in the air. Cut precisely on the inside of your markings with the Japanese saw's rip-cut side. Be careful that the cut is vertical, and saw down the whole depth on both sides.

6. Position the wood piece on the work surface so the slot lies against the underlay. Lay a flat sheet you aren't worried about underneath if you don't want to risk damaging the work surface; secure the piece again. Use a chisel narrower or the same width as the slot. It should not be wider.

7. Use the chisel to first chip away the fibers from the top down on the slot's bottom marking. Then, chip away the bit from the end side of the wood. Do only a little at a time. Continue until you have gone all the way through. Always keep the tapered side of the chisel turned toward the waste wood.

8. When you've chipped away the waste wood, clean the bottom with the chisel so it's completely flat, and then finesse the slot and tongue if necessary. Use the chisel or a file.

9. Make sure that the joint fits together well.

10. Spread glue on the contact surfaces and clamp together. Place a small piece of wood, cork, or something similar between the wood and clamp so you don't leave press marks on the wood. Double check the right angle with a try square.

Inset Fittings

If you want a hanging fitting or hinge that will join together with a piece of wood, you must inset them. In principle, you do this the same way as for all fittings, adapted to the shape of the fitting. Here, I show how you can inset a hanger plate. There are many types of hanger plates. The type I use most often is one that looks like a keyhole.

1. Lay the fitting on the desired place on your piece of wood and trace the contours and holes.

2. Bore the corners with a wood bore of the same diameter as the rounding on the fitting. In this case, it's ½ inch (12 mm). Bore so that the hole aligns precisely on the edge with the line. The depth of the hole should be about $\frac{1}{32}$–$\frac{1}{16}$ inch (1–2 mm) deeper than the thickness of the fitting. Use a chisel about ⅜–⅝ inch (10–16 mm) wide to chip along the straight line, with the flat side of the chisel turned outward. Chip as deep as the hole.

3. Cut away the material between the two holes with the chisel so you have an even surface. It does not matter if it's neat, since it'll never be seen.

4. Place the fitting and draw the "keyhole." Keep in mind that the narrower part will be turned upward.

5. Precisely bore two holes next to each other over your marking with a wood bore that is a couple of millimeters larger than the large part of the hole—in this case a $\frac{3}{8}$ inch (10 mm) bore. Bore about $\frac{13}{64}$–$\frac{3}{8}$ inch (5–10 mm) deep. Then, chip away the material between the hole so you have an elongated hole.

6. Pick all the shavings out of the hole and then screw the fitting on. Don't forget that the narrow part of the "keyhole" should be turned upward.

FILES AND RASPS

Rounding an edge or a round dowel is easiest with a rasp and file. They are very worthwhile tools because they can help make straight and rounded shapes. Consider both the file and rasp as cutting tools. They cut only when you push the tool forward (if you have the handle toward yourself). When filing or rasping, you should also hold the tool against the wood, push it away, and then lift it up from the wood before the next push. If you don't lift it up but, instead, pull it across the wood, even on the way back, you'll diminish the sharpness of the tool. You should regularly brush the file and rasp with a file brush—a thin metal brush that removes compressed wood dust that has embedded between the tracks.

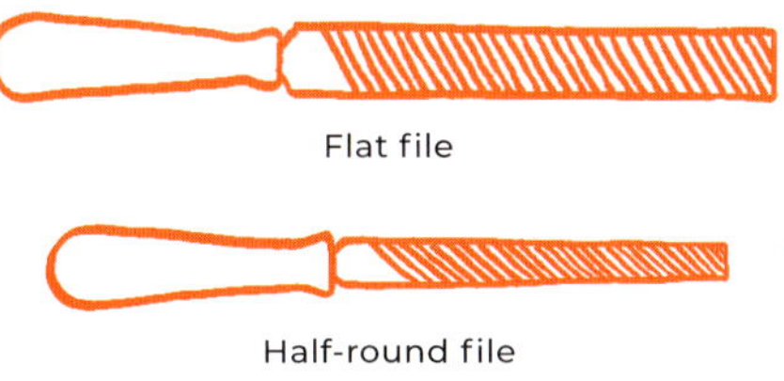

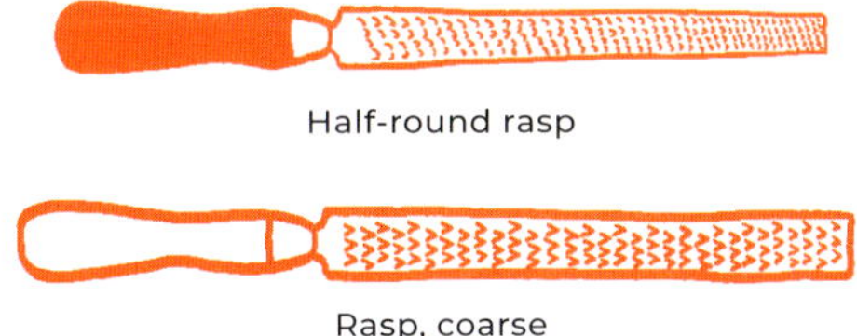

File

A file has fine metal teeth called burrs, diagonally set on the blade. There are various degrees of coarseness, but I think a medium-coarse file is sufficient. Still, it can be good to have choices, such as a flat file, a half-round file, and a round file. The flat file is good for filing flat surfaces, the half round for concave and convex shapes, and a round file for filing up holes or filing in smaller rounded areas.

Rasp

Rasps are coarser than files and have more cutting burrs like small teeth. The most useful rasp is a half-round one with a flat side and a half-round side. It can make both concave and convex shapes. A rasp is for rough shaving and produces rather deep scratches in the wood, so make sure to change to a file when you have only a little material left to shave off.

Rounding Dowels

1. Mark the center on the end of a dowel. Draw concentric circles on the end, spaced about $^{13}/_{64}$ inch (5 mm) apart. Use a compass or a circle template.

2. Draw lines around the dowel. The lowest line should be the same distance from the end as the length of the dowel's radius. Use a finger from the hand you hold a pencil in as a support against the end. Hold the pencil tip on the desired spot of the dowel and then twist the dowel around until you've drawn a line all around the dowel.

3. Make couple more markings around the dowel. Make a template in paper or cardboard in the shape of a quarter circle, with the same radius as the dowel.

4. Secure the dowel so that the end you'll work on sticks out from the work surface. Place a piece of cork or a similar soft bit between the clamp and the dowel to avoid press marks. Begin rasping the edge of the dowel, following your markings so you know that you're shaving off the same amount all around. Begin with the first circle and then the next. You should turn the dowel a few times so you can go all the way around.

5. Check often against the template to be sure you're not shaving off too much. When you're close to the finished rounding, change to the file. File until you're finished and then file away any tracks made by the rasp. Use the template to check to make sure you haven't filed away too much.

6. Finish with sandpaper without a sanding block. Begin with a somewhat coarser sandpaper (about 150 grit) and then finer (about 240 grit).

NAILS AND MANDRELS

Most often, one doesn't use nails these days; screws of various types are used instead. Nevertheless, I think that a nailhead can be a fine detail even if nailing isn't perhaps the most elegant construction solution. There are many different kinds of nails for various purposes. I have listed the most common nails for woodworking and the related tools below.

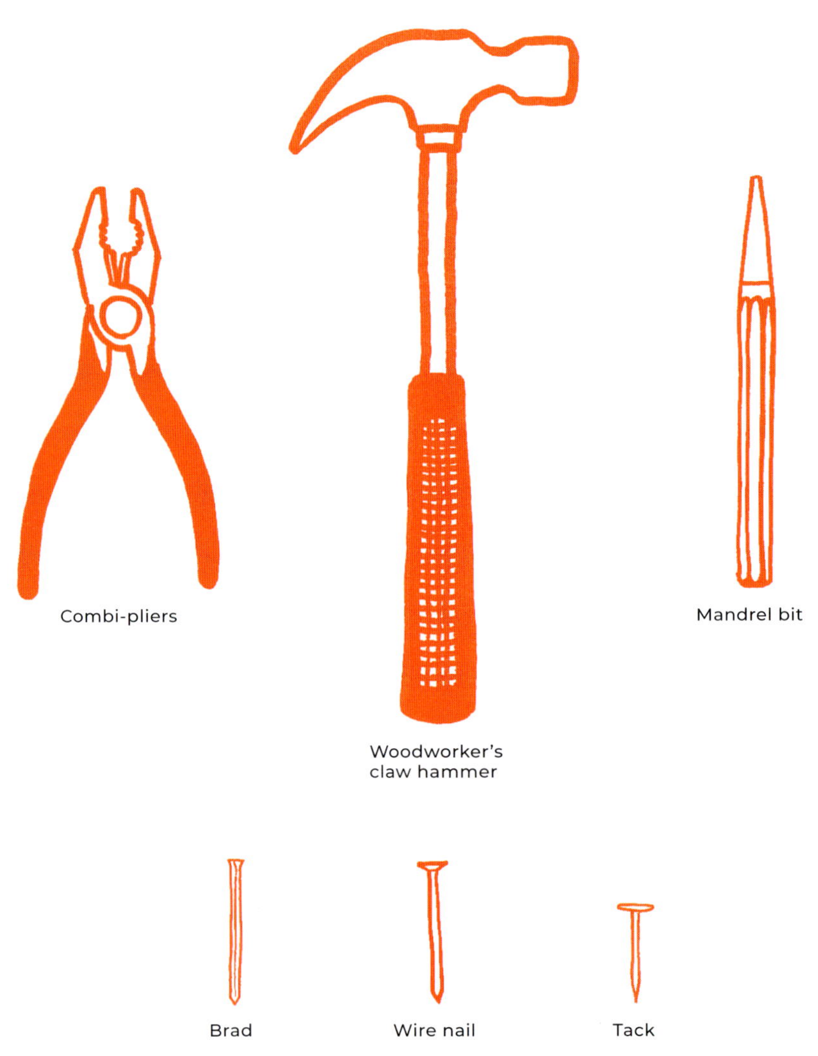

Carpenter's Claw Hammer

A claw hammer has a steel shaft and a claw on the back of the head to pull up nails. These hammers come in many different sizes, and I recommend one of the smaller ones for cabinetry. Make sure that the hammerhead is clean—a dirty head can easily smudge the piece of wood you're hammering.

Mandrel Bit

These are used to avoid leaving marks from the hammer when you're going to hammer a nail down at or below the wood surface.

Combi-Pliers

Combi-pliers are pliers with combined jaws and grooved grippers outermost and forceps innermost. All-around pliers that can be used for almost anything—good to have in the toolbox!

Wire Nail

Wire nails are made of metal thread—hence the name—with a flat or conical head. It's the most common type of nail for joining wood. There are many different kinds, sizes, and metals.

Brad

Nails with small heads and often grooved surface for a better grip. There are many different kinds and sizes, and they are most often used for furniture carpentry, such as moldings and linings. The head is driven into the wood surface with a mandrel bit.

Tack

A tack is a shorter nail, approximately 5⁄16–5⁄8 inch (8–16 mm) with a flat head.

Removing a Nail

If you need to pull out a nail, do so with the claw on the back of the hammerhead or pliers. Place a wood block or disc beneath the hammer or pliers when you pull up to avoid press marks on the wood.

Nailing Near the Edge

If you're going to hammer in a nail near the edge or end wood, you risk splitting the wood. To avoid that, you can clip the point off the nail or hammer it so it's blunt. This will decrease the chances of splitting the wood. If that doesn't help, you can pre-bore through the top layer of wood with a bore with the same or smaller diameter than the nail.

Hammering In Short Nails

1. When you need to hammer in short nails or brads, it can be difficult to get a grip on them with your fingers. Instead, use pliers for gripping.

2. Hold the pliers against the piece of wood and hammer with a couple of hits until the nail is stuck in the wood.

3. Remove the pliers and hammer in the rest of the nail. Hold the hammer outermost on the shaft and hit the nail so the strike comes straight down from above; otherwise, the nail will go in crooked. Look at the nail as you hammer.

4. To prevent the hammer from leaving a mark on the wood, you can hammer in the last step with a mandrel. Hold the mandrel completely straight over the nailhead and make a couple of direct hits with the hammer. The nailhead should land just under or in line with the wood surface.

BORING AND SCREWING

If you're going to screw two pieces of wood together, you'll almost always need to begin by pre-boring into the top piece and sometimes into the lower piece, depending on the type of screw and wood layers. The hole in the top piece of wood should have the same diameter as the outer measurement of the screw's threads, so that the screw will go into the hole without catching its threads. The hole in the lower piece of wood should have the same or slightly smaller diameter than the inner measurement of the threads so that the screw catches without splitting the wood.

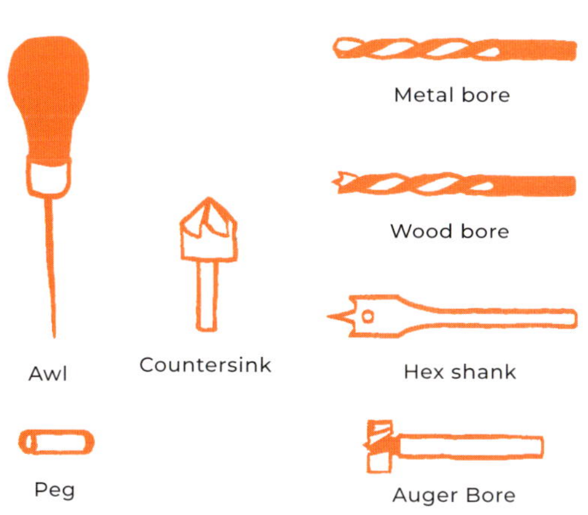

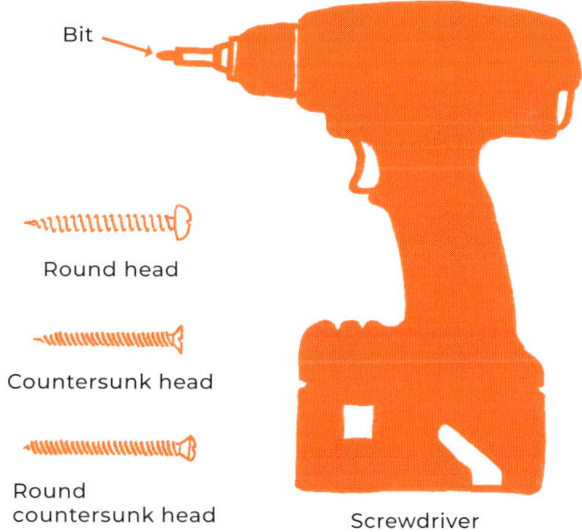

Screws

The variety of available screws is endless! There are screws for anything you can think of to screw together, and the uses are quite clear on the packaging. For wood screws, there are three types of head to be familiar with.

Countersunk Head

The most common wood screw has a countersunk (recessed) head. The countersunk head is screwed down into the wood so the top lies aligned with the surface of the wood. It's a good idea to test screw in a piece of wood before countersinking the holes, to make sure how much the head is drawn down into the wood by just screwing it in. Then, check the depth of the countersinking after that.

Round Head

Roundhead screws are used for mounting fittings that don't have countersunk holes, and are even good to use when you want to be able to screw properly without the head going into the wood, such as, for example, when you're placing a wood plug over the screw.

Round Countersunk Head

These are used when the screw should be more decorative; for example, for fittings, but also for screwing together pieces of wood with a visible head. A personal favorite is a brass screw with a round countersunk head. Countersink in the wood so the sunken part of the screw lands under the surface of the wood and the round part sticks up above.

Awl

An awl is a pointed metal stick with a shaft for marking the wood to make it easier to guide in a screw or nail. Either press at the desired spot by hand or lightly hit with a wood mallet on the shaft.

Peg

A peg or pin is a round bit of dowel in a hardwood such as beech or birch that you use when you want to join two pieces of wood rigidly against each other. It's grooved and beveled so the glue will have some place to run when you drive it into the hole, which prevents the wood from splitting and so the glue can be evenly distributed.

Boring

When you're boring, it's important that the bore steel comes up quickly before you press it down against the wood. You can hold it so the peg touches the wood. If you press the steel down against the wood piece before it quickly comes up, there is a great risk that the wood will chip.

Screwdriver

A screwdriver is a must-have in my toolbox. It's probably the tool you'll use most, and so it's worth buying a good-quality screwdriver. For a hobby carpenter, the most expensive ones are not necessary, but still, you should buy a good brand. If you want to use the same machine for both boring and screwing, I think an 18-volt model is best. It's strong enough for screwing and boring on most cabinetry without being too awkward.

Most screwdrivers have two speeds. Generally, you'll work at speed 1 when you're screwing, and speed 2 for boring. Speed 1 is slower, which gives you better control and diminishes the risk of driving the screw in too deep or damaging the screw's path with the bit. Speed 2 is faster, which is often necessary for boring because the bore steel should have time to cut through the material.

Bits

Bits are interchangeable screwdriver heads for certain types of screw chisels. If you're going to use bits in a screwdriver, you should also use a bit holder. Screw packets always list which bits should be used with them, and the bit model will be either marked on the bit or at its hole in the bit box. Always return bits to the correct place in the bit box. Be careful to use the correct bit for the screw. If you use the wrong one, either the screw or bit will quickly wear out and be unusable.

Wood Bore

Wood bores are spiral-shaped and have a center spike. The center spike holds it in place, and it's easy to set the spike precisely where you want a hole.

Metal Bore

Metal bores are spiral-shaped and good for smaller holes. They do not have a center spike but, instead, are conical at the end. For that reason, you should make a mark with an awl before you bore, so the point has a guide. Of course, you can also use a larger metal bore for wood, but the risk of shifting position is also somewhat greater.

Auger Bore

For boring larger holes, it's best to use an auger bore. They have a small center spike and fine cutting to prevent fraying and to make a sharp cut. It's a little heavier to bore with an auger because it does not cut the wood as quickly as a center bore, but the results are much better. Also, because the auger has a body, it's much easier to hold straight as you work.

Hex-Shank Flat-Spade Wood Drill Bore

A hex-shank flat-spade wood drill bore is flat with a centered spike and two cutting blades. It's suitable for coarser kinds of woodworking without much finesse. Personally, I think that it's difficult to bore good holes with a flat-spade bore when using a screwdriver. They function better with a pillar drill, which holds the angle. Because a flat-spade bore is flat, it can be difficult to hold it at the right angle because the body on the bore steel does not guide into the hole. In addition, the wood easily flakes because the cut is most often rather large.

Countersink

You'll countersink before screwing in a screw with a countersunk or round countersunk head, so that the screwhead lands at the desired depth without splitting the wood. A countersink comes in a variety of sizes and angles, but I think it's sufficient to have one in a standard size.

Boring Straight

To make it easier to see that you're holding the bore vertically, you can set a try square next to it. That way, you'll see that the spacing is even throughout the boring.

If you're going to bore to a specific depth, you can measure the depth on the bore steel and place a bit of masking tape around the steel as a marker. There are also bore stops, metal bits that are slipped on and secure the bore steel to the desired depth.

Countersinking

Always match the depth of the sinking to the size of the screwhead that will be screwed into the hole. Hold the countersink as perpendicular as you can. If you hold it crooked, the sinking will be uneven.

Joining with Pegs

1. Mark the spot on the wood piece where you want to bore a hole for a peg. Emphasize the mark with an awl so the bore will have a guiding hole.

2. Measure the depth of the bore bit and place a bit of tape as a marker. The total depth of both holes should be slightly longer (a couple of millimeters) than the peg. Secure the wood and then bore with a wood bore at your markings. Bore as perpendicular as you can.

3. Place a marking pin in the hole and press against the other bit. If you don't have any marking pins, you can measure the hole on the other bit also, but it's important that the measurement be exact; otherwise, the holes won't match.

4. Secure the second piece and bore at the marks from the marking pin. Work as for step 3.

Without glue, test to make sure that the elements match (this is called a "dry gluing"). It can be difficult to make a hole that matches perfectly when you do it by hand and there is not the smallest room for tiny adjustments. If they don't go together because the pegs don't fit, you can carve or file a little on the holes or pegs where they are off. Be careful that you don't remove too much material. If everything then fits together, all you have left to do is to glue.

5. Put some wood glue in the hole and on the contact surfaces of both bits. Sweep around the hole with a thin stick or pencil so that the glue is spread throughout the hole.

Drive the peg into the hole on one bit with a wooden mallet. Tap it in until it hits the bottom of the hole. You can hear the sound when it hits the bottom, since it will sound more muted. If you don't hear any difference, measure to make sure the peg has gone to the same depth as the hole was bored.

Securely hit in the other bit with a wooden mallet; place a block or something similar in between to avoid hit marks.

6. Clamp the pieces to be glued and make sure that the press is centered over the glue surface.

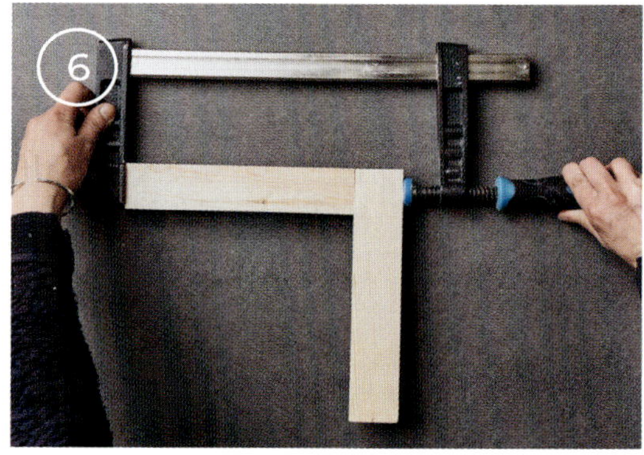

Wood Plugs over Screws

Screwing and then hiding the screw-head with a wood plug is an easy and fine construction. You can make it more or less visible, depending on what type of wood you choose for the wood plug and in what direction you decide to place the grain. You can make a wood plug from a dowel, or you can bore one in your choice of wood with a so-called tap drill. To screw with a wood plug is nice in places where it can be difficult to put pressure, or if you're making a piece of furniture but don't have clamps with a deep enough gap to press the wood pieces together. Because you first glue and then screw the construction together, pushing on the glue joint will be sufficient. Place the screws a maximum of 6 inches (150 mm) apart.

1. Prepare the material you're going to use. Saw a dowel and bevel the plugs a little at one end. Mark where you want the holes.

Bore at your marks with a bore of the same diameter as the wood plugs, which will be glued in. If you're using a plug smaller than ½ inch (12 mm) in diameter, you should use a wood bore. If it's larger than ½ inch (12 mm), use an auger bore. Bore down to about half the thickness of the wood piece.

2. Bore the last bit in with a bore that is the same diameter as the screw.

3. Put the wood glue on the contact surfaces and then screw the wood pieces together. Use a screw with a round head. Let the glue dry and then go over all the screws once more and test to see if they need to be screwed in a bit more.

4. Put some glue in the plug hole and then drive in the wood plug, with the beveled side downward. Think about which direction you want the grain before you drive it in. Hit with a wood mallet and make sure that you hit it in all the way down to the screwhead.

5. Let the glue dry and then saw off the tap that sticks up, using a Japanese saw or flush saw.

6. File, cut, or grind off the last bits of material on the plug until it's completely even with the piece of wood. Finish the grinding with fine sandpaper.

CARVING

When doing woodwork for yourself, I think it can be very fine to get an extra feeling of the handmade. Carving in details such as knobs or making an edge with a carving knife instead of grinding says, "I made it with my own hands." It's also very fine to combine a crafted look with something a little more carefully carved.

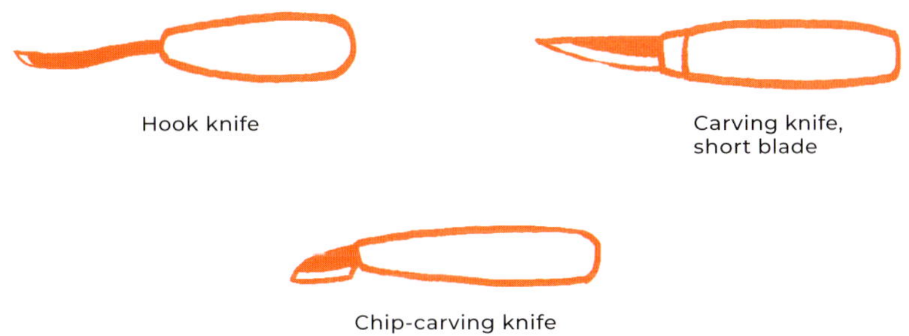

Hook Knife

A hook knife has a V-shaped blade with two straight edges, and it's used for cutting in patterns and letters. Be extra careful with the edges on a hook knife, since they are fragile and hard to keep sharp.

Carving Knife

A carving knife has a short blade, about 2 inches (50 mm) long, which makes it flexible to handle and gives control over the cutting. There are many fine handmade variations, but even cheaper commercial ones also function well. Just make sure to keep the knife sharp and be leery of the edges. That goes for all cutting tools. It's never good to carve with a dull knife. Keep it in its case when you aren't using it, and use another knife for coarse carving.

Chip-Carving Knife

Just like a carving knife, a chip-carving knife has an edged blade, but the blade is shaped for cutting patterns in wood rather than carving. Chip-carving knives come in many different variations, with the blade usually about ⅝–2 inches (15–50 mm) long. Be extra vigilant of the point on a chip knife because it's the one you'll use the most.

Edging with a Knife

In general, you should always carve following the grain of the wood. You'll quickly feel if you're carving in the wrong direction because the knife will catch in the wood. Keep track of all your fingers, so nothing is in the path of the edge in case you slip. Begin with small careful strokes, when you have the hang of it, and get a sense of how this piece of wood feels so you can begin to make more targeted cuts, continuing, of course, carefully and with total control.

The easiest and most useful carving technique is to hold the knife in your carving hand near the blade and to press on the back of the blade with the thumb of your other hand. With this grip, you can have good control over both the blade and how much you remove. When you're carving end wood, the same applies, but keep in mind that the end wood is harder to carve and so you'll need to make smaller cuts for good results. Also be careful when you cut against the corners of the end wood because you can easily make chips if you're not carving carefully or turning direction and carving off the corner from the other direction.

GLUING

It's a very critical moment when you're about to glue together a piece of furniture you've made. You have only one chance, and it cannot go wrong. For that reason, it's important to prepare the gluing as well as possible and have everything you need beforehand.

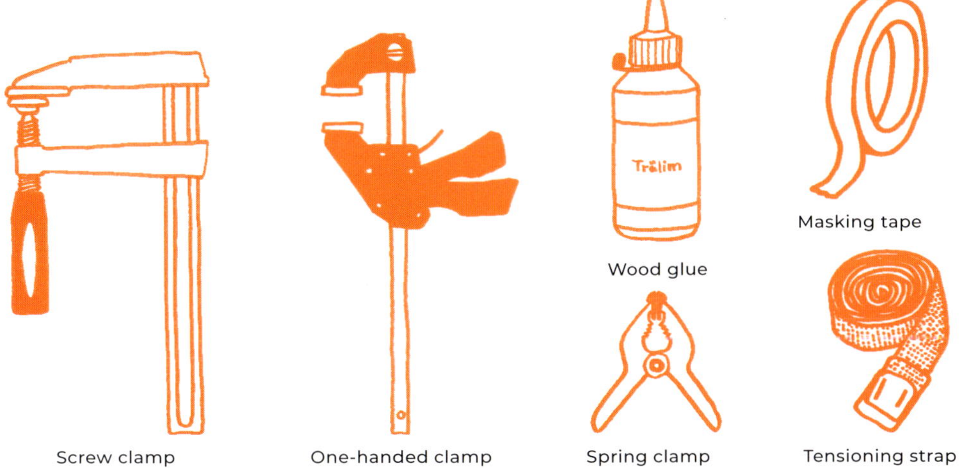

Screw Clamp

For fine carpentry, the screw clamp is the most common clamp. You can lock and tension it by pressing up on the lower jaw so it's against the piece of wood, and then tension it with a handle on the set screw. This type of clamp is available in several sizes and styles, and the truth is that you can't have too many clamps, preferably in a variety of sizes. When you're clamping, the clamp's jaw must lie flat against the piece of wood and in a straight line with the press, parallel to the wood. Otherwise, the pressure will make the joint crooked or allow it to glide out of position.

One-Handed Clamp

A one-handed clamp tensions by being pumped on a handle. Precisely as its name implies, it's both tensioned and loosened with only one hand. It's smooth to work with, but it does not have as large a cap and does not tension as firmly as a screw clamp. If you're going to glue something that is wider than the gap on your largest clamp, you can do a series connection with two clamps by securely hooking the top two jaws of the clamps to each other and then clamping. This works for all clamps but functions best with one-handed clamps.

Spring Clamp

A spring clamp is stronger clamp that's used when you want to glue smaller pieces that don't need much pressure. A spring clamp is also good for clamping different parts together; for example, when assembling.

Tensioning Strap

You can find straps either with buckle or locking tensioning. These are good for gluing miters, frames, and similar items. The buckle style strap gives you good pressure; just be sure to protect the wood with a disc or thin block because it can easily be marked.

Masking Tape

Masking tape is paper tape with low adhesion that is primarily for covering surfaces when painting. However, masking tape is good to have on hand when woodworking, partly to mark pieces and to mark depth on a bore, but most of all, to use for tensioning when you're gluing. If, for example, you're going to glue a chip that fell off an edge or to make a small repair, then masking tape can't be beat. You only tension it over the glued area, so the tape holds it in place. The pressure from the tension in the tape is often enough for this little bit of gluing.

Wood Glue

The most common type of glue used for furniture carpentry is water-based PVA glue. It comes in both interior and exterior glues. They usually have a hardening time of about 10–15 minutes; read the instruction label on the bottle. With PVA glue, you can glue wood, sheet materials, textiles, and paper. It's not dangerous if you get it on your skin, and it easily washes off with water.

Dry Gluing

It's always a good idea to go through a dry gluing before you actually glue something. This means that you join the wood pieces exactly as you would for gluing, using clamps, tension blocks, etc., although you'll do it without glue. This way, you'll go through the entire procedure and can note any problems that pop up and so you'll know which pieces to join first. Once you've done the dry gluing, then you can do the actual gluing!

Glue Join

1. Lay the pieces so the annual rings on the end wood are aligned as shown in the drawing below.

When they are aligned in the correct order, you can draw a triangle on the topside with a pencil. Draw lightly so the lines can easily be erased later.

2. You'll need four tensioning blocks and two spacing blocks, all the same length as the total width of the glue join. The tension blocks should be thick enough so they won't fail—they must be able to hold the glue join straight. The spacing blocks should be about ¾–1³⁄16 inches (20–30 mm) high, so you can insert the jaw with a clamp underneath.

Place packing tape on the side with the tensioning blocks and the spacing blocks that will be turned toward the glue join. You'll do this so the blocks won't be glued into the glue join by the glue that will be squeezed out between the joins.

3. Lay the pieces in the correct order on the spacing blocks and turn them up on their high edge. Turn all of them up in the same direction.

4. Squirt the glue out onto the edges and spread the glue with your fingers so it's spread out evenly. Don't glue the edges that will be turned outward. Turn the pieces down and make sure that the triangle aligns.

5. Place two or more clamps, depending on how large of a glue join sheet you're making. The clamps should be spaced about 6–8 inches (150–200 mm) apart. The press should be in a straight line, centered on the join. Tension to about half of what's needed, only tightly enough to hold the pieces in place and so the clamps sit firmly.

6. Next, tighten the tension blocks firmly with tape turned to the glue join, straight across the glue join on both ends. There should be a block on both the top and bottom sides. Firmly clamp these with two or three clamps per end, two at the corners, and one in the middle. Now, tension the clamps completely on the glue join. Let dry.

Gluing a Miter

The easiest way to glue a miter on—for example, a frame—is with a tensioning strap or tape. Tape is easy and smooth if you're going to glue only a small piece. For larger pieces that need more tension, it's better to use a tensioning strap.

Gluing with Masking Tape

1. Lay the pieces with the miter ends against each other in a row, with the outer side upmost. Place tape strips over every join. The wider the piece, the more tape strips.

2. Spread glue on the contact surfaces of the joins.

3. Turn the sides up, so the tape will tighten and add tension at the corners.

4. Tape the last join last, once you've joined the side. Tighten the tape a little, so the join will be tight. Use a try square to ascertain that the corner is at a 90° angle.

Gluing with a Tension Strap

1. Begin by taping precisely as in step 1, on the previous page, to hold the pieces in place. Glue and then place the tensioning strap around the glued pieces; the amount depends on how big the pieces to be glued together are. Tighten the strap as much as you can by hand.

2. Wedge wooden blocks between the strap and the piece being glued, with the width facing the piece.

3. Now twist the wooden blocks one after the other on end until the strap cannot be tensioned any further. Wedge in as many and as wide blocks as necessary. This varies depending on the size of the item you're gluing. Just keep in mind not to use this technique if you're going to glue narrow pieces, because the sides can flex inward from the pressure of the blocks.

If you use a tensioning strap with a buckle, you should only pull it in until the glue looks firm. Place a thin piece of wood or cork beneath the strap so it won't leave a mark from the metal on the wood.

SANDING

Sanding is one of the last steps you take to smooth out the joins, break the edges (to round the edges with a chisel, a file, or sandpaper), and achieve fine surfaces before it's time for surface finishing.

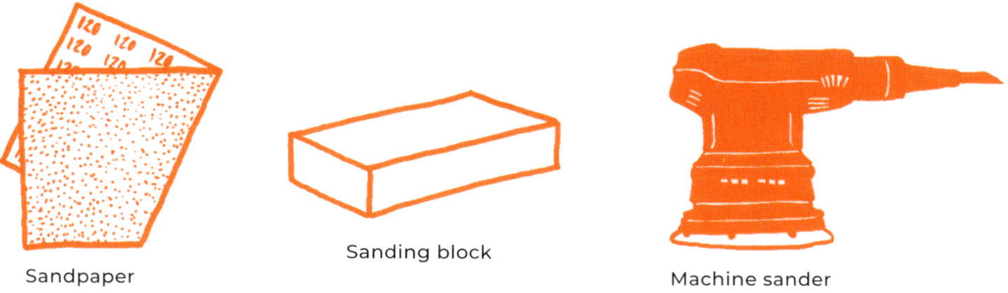

Sandpaper

Sanding block

Machine sander

Sandpaper

You can find many different grit sizes of sandpaper from about 12 to 800. The degree of coarseness is marked on the backside of the paper. The higher the number, the finer the grit. For cabinetry, you'll normally use only sandpaper between 80 and 400. There is sandpaper with the grit firmly on the paper, and sanding cloth with the grit on a textile. In my experience, the sanding cloth has a longer lifespan, but sandpaper works better for corners and joins.

Sanding Blocks

A cork block is used to sand flat surfaces and edges.

Machine Sander

If you, like me, think that sanding is the most boring part of carpentry, it would be worthwhile to own a machine sander. I prefer an orbital sander—it's the easiest machine to handle and is versatile. Simply said, it spins and vibrates at the same time. It has a round plate with a burr pad that you attach to the sandpaper, so it's easy to change paper.

The big difference from sanding by hand is that the machine makes it much faster. The disadvantage is that it makes it hard to see what has and has not been sanded. Unfortunately, if you hold the sander still in one place, it quickly makes a pit in the surface. You can draw a few light pencil lines on the wood surface and then sand until the lines disappear from the entire surface, so you'll have an even sanding. I do not recommend breaking the edges and sanding end wood with a machine sander. It seldom works well because you have so little control. For a better result, sand these areas by hand. You should also think about the dust and noise from the machine—use hearing and respiratory protection. The same grit sizes apply to a machine sander as for hand sanding.

Sanding a Flat Surface with a Block

Always sand following the wood grain. Use a cork sanding block to achieve an even surface. The sandpaper should be the same length as the block and wide enough to go over the edges so you can get a good grip on it. Go from coarse paper to finer. The size grit you begin with depends on how coarse the surface is at the beginning. Do not make too big a jump in grit sizes. If, for example, you go directly from 120 to 240 grit, it'll take a long time to remove the tracks of the coarser paper. You'll save time and energy by sanding with 180 grit in between.

Sanding a Flat Surface without a Block

Surfaces that are difficult to sand with a block can be sanded with sandpaper directly in your hand, a method I use if I want to have a purposely uneven surface. You can also sand without a block when you're only going to break the fibers on the wood with a very fine-grit sandpaper, such as, for example, after surface work.

Breaking Edges

When using a sanding block for breaking edges on wood, you can get a sharp bevel. With a wooden block, the bevel will be even sharper than if you use a cork block. For a rounder appearance, it's better to sand the edge without a block, instead holding the paper right in your hand. The paper then conforms to your fingers, and the bevel will be softer. The coarser the sandpaper, the bigger the bevel will be. I use sandpaper between 180 and 320 grit, depending on how much I want to sand off. How much to break your edges is a completely individual choice, so do what you think will be the nicest.

Dividing Sandpaper

You can buy sandpaper in sheets or in a roll. Most often, it's in a larger format than is easy to handle, so you'll likely need to divide the paper to fit, for example, on a sanding block. You should not cut or snip sandpaper, or your work tool will become dull! When you need to divide a sheet of sandpaper, tear it to the desired size. To tear it evenly and straight, lay the paper with the grit downward and then lay something sharp, such as a steel ruler, over it. Hold the ruler steady against the paper and tear along the edge of the ruler. If you have coarser sandpaper, it's a good idea to first fold the paper at the desired place so it'll be easier to tear. Always divide the paper into perpendicular pieces.

Folding Sandpaper

When you want to sand without a block, you should fold the sandpaper for better control. First, fold it on one side, a third of the way in from the edge, and then fold the other side over your first turn. This is the most material-effective way to fold sandpaper. You can use both sides until they are worn out. When one side is worn out, you just have to fold up the underside and put it on top instead.

SURFACE FINISHING

To my mind, oil makes the finest surface finish for furniture. It gives the wood deep protection and becomes very beautiful with age. However, keep in mind that linseed-soaked rags, paper, and sponges can self-ignite if you leave them out. This seldom happens, but it can. Always make sure to soak or burn used rags. If you want to use them again, they should be stored in a jar with a tight lid.

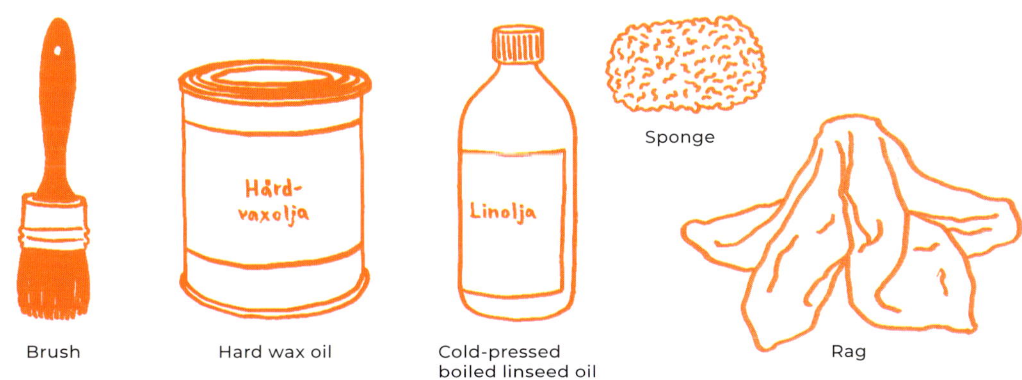

Cold-Pressed Boiled Linseed Oil

Cold-pressed boiled linseed oil is processed from flax seeds. Very good linseed oils are produced in Sweden. Linseed oil hardens by oxidizing, which means that the oil hardens when in contact with oxygen. It's difficult to say how long it takes for linseed oil to harden, because it depends on the humidity in the air and the temperature. For the best results, you should oil your furniture when it's warm and well ventilated.

Apply an even layer of oil, let it soak into the wood for about 20–30 minutes, and then wipe away any excess oil. Linseed oil is excellent for finishing the surfaces of both indoor and outdoor furniture. You can use water and soap to easily wash off any linseed oil. Usually, linseed oil is thinned with turpentine or white spirit to make hardening faster, so you'll have quicker results. I recommend that you leave the oil as is and let it dry in its own time.

Hard Wax Oil

Hard wax oil is a mixture of different oils and waxes that are used, in many cases, for oiling flooring but are also very popular for furniture carpentry. Hard wax oil penetrates the wood and, at the same time, adds a protective layer to the surface that is water- and dirt-repellent. It's only intended for interior use. Hard wax oil comes in many variations—natural, pigmented, and a range of glossiness. They can each have different drying times, so read the information on the can label and follow the advice.

Hard wax oil can be difficult to remove from your hands, so it's a good idea to wear gloves when using it. If you forget, as I sometimes do, you can remove most of it from your hands by first dipping them in linseed oil to loosen up the wax and then washing off the linseed oil with soap.

Surface Finishing with Oil or Hard Wax Oil

You can use a brush, rag, or sponge to apply oil to wood. Spread the oil onto the piece of wood, following the wood grain. It's easy to maintain your oiled furniture by just adding a new layer if the surface is showing wear or is dry. Just make sure to wash the surface before oiling and, if necessary, sand it lightly with fine sandpaper.

Brush

I think brushing on boiled linseed oil works well for outdoor furniture. This is partly because the surface is often a bit coarser than on indoor furniture, and a sponge or rag can snag on the wood fibers. Also, brushing makes the application more fluid, and furniture that will be outside needs a lot of oil. The disadvantage with a brush is that it's more difficult to control the amount of oil, which can then run easily. Don't forget to wash the brush, either in a brush wash or, if using linseed oil, with soap and water.

Rags

Rags are good for using on indoor furniture and work well both for linseed oil and hard wax oil. A rag gives you good control over a fair amount of oil, and it's easy to apply and get into the corners. It's hard to avoid oily hands, though, so wear gloves. You'll find various kinds of rags to use, such as linen rags, cotton rags, or dishcloths.

The fibers in linen rags polish the surface a little as you oil, which is very nice. However, they are not very absorbent.

Cotton rags, on the other hand, are absorbent and polish the wood a bit, but not in the same way as linen rags. They work well both for applying oil and wiping away any excess oil.

Dishcloths have the best absorbency, and most people already have some on hand. I still recommend using either linen or cotton rags for oiling because dishcloths can easily snag on the wood if it's the least bit chipped, and then it can be hard to remove the fiber bits left by the dishcloth.

Sponges

Sponges—either natural or synthetic sponges—are most suitable for oiling indoor furniture because they have similar qualities. Sponges can hold a lot of oil without dripping, and it's easy to control how much you apply to the wood. However, the same disadvantages apply to sponges as to dishrags—they can easily catch on small bits of wood fiber, so make sure that you have a well-sanded surface if you're applying oil with a sponge. Soft sponges have no polishing effect, but their scrubbing side can polish.

In-Between Sanding

When the oil or hard wax oil has dried, you can do a so-called in-between sanding. You can do this by sanding down the wood fibers left when you applied the first layer of oil. Sand lightly with fine sandpaper, 320 or 400 grit. Then oil the furniture again, the same way as for the first layer.

PROJECTS

On the following pages, you'll find 20 projects for home and garden—some for inside your house and others for the garden or balcony. You'll use the knowledge of techniques and tools you learned in the previous chapter.

Explanation of the Illustrations

The measurements for all drawings are in inches.

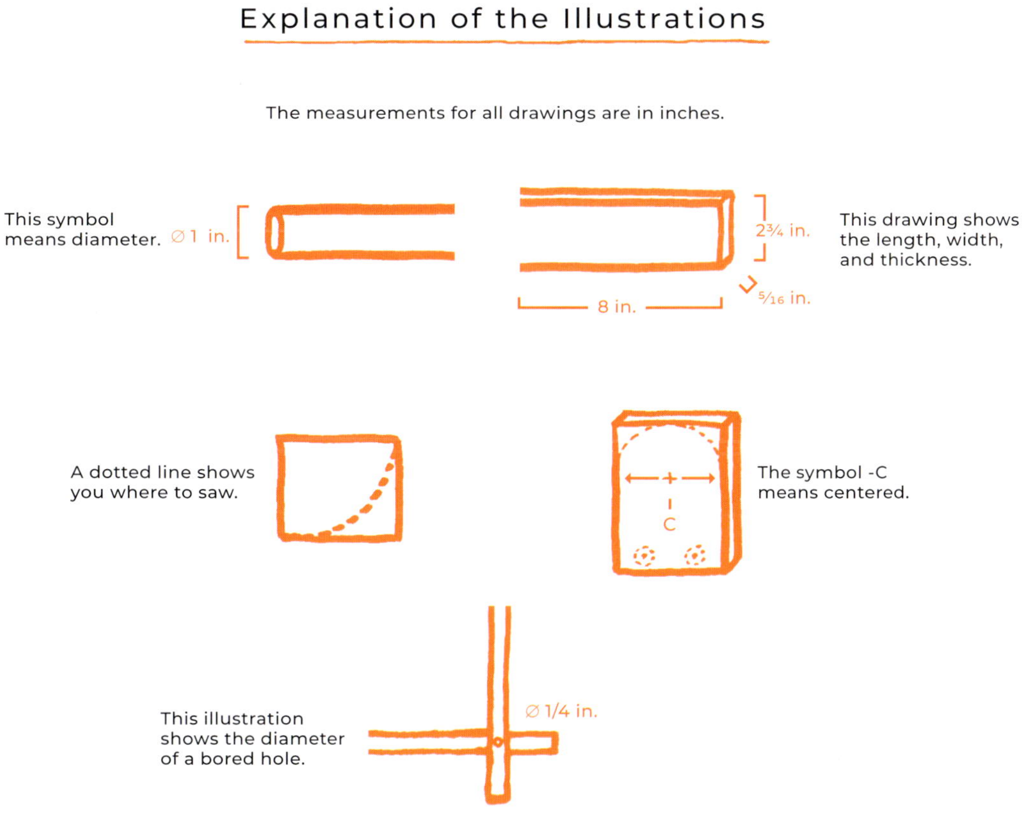

JAPURA
PRIMA
GARANTERAS
REN

SPICE RACK

The spice jars in my kitchen are always stashed higgledy-piggledy in a cupboard. I usually have to move at least five jars before I find the right one, and this happens every time I cook. I'm certainly not the only person with this problem! So I made a spice rack with a basic shelf wide enough to hold standard-size spice jars two deep. It's a simple construction that can be adapted in shape and size for your kitchen.

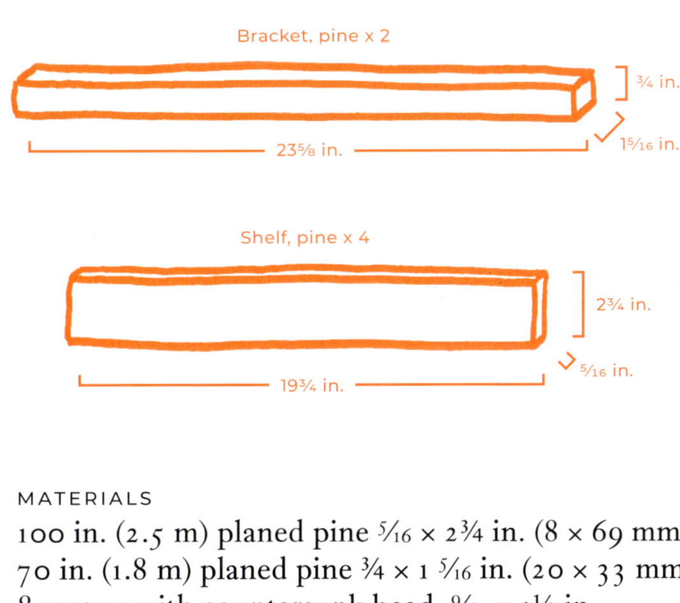

TOOLS

Folding rule
Japanese saw
Clamp
Sandpaper, 120 and 240
Sanding block
Wood chisel ⁵⁄₁₆ in. (8 mm)
Wood bore ⅛, ⅜, and ⁹⁄₁₆ in. (3, 10, and 14 mm)
Screwdriver with bits
Countersink
Wooden mallet
Miter box
Brush or sponge

MATERIALS

100 in. (2.5 m) planed pine ⁵⁄₁₆ × 2¾ in. (8 × 69 mm)
70 in. (1.8 m) planed pine ¾ × 1 ⁵⁄₁₆ in. (20 × 33 mm)
8 screws with countersunk head, ⁹⁄₆₄ × 1½ in. (3.5 × 40 mm)
2 hanger plates
4 screws with countersunk head ³⁄₃₂ × ¾ in. (2.5 × 20 mm)
Wood glue
Boiled linseed oil

STEP 1 Measure and cut material, following drawings on previous page. Use the Japanese saw and a miter box.

STEP 2 Sand the cut surfaces with sandpaper. Use a sanding block so the edges won't be rounded—they need a sharp finish.

STEP 3 Mark where each shelf will sit on the front of the brackets (see measurements in illustration below). The markings should be the same thickness as the shelves. Then, draw a line for the depth on the cutouts on both sides of the respective bracket. They should go down ⅔ of the thickness or ¾ inch (20 mm). Use a try square.

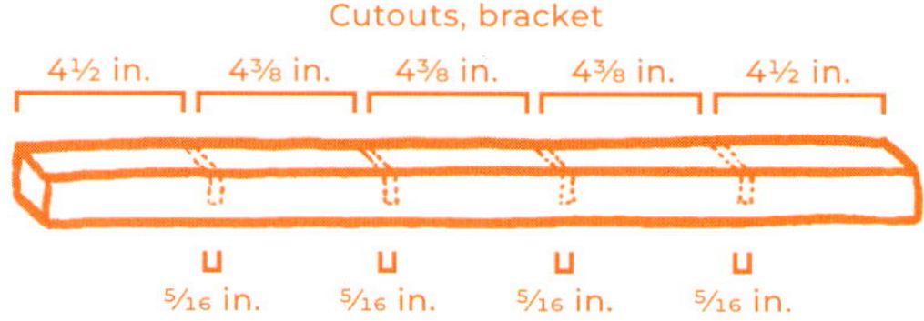

STEP 4 Securely tension one of the brackets to the work surface. Cut inside the markings with the Japanese saw. If you cut outside the line, the cutouts will be too big. It's better to use a block for support. Cut down to the markings. Make sure that you cut to the same length down on both sides. Repeat the same procedure on the remaining seven markings on the bracket.

STEP 5 Chip away any material between the saw cuts on the brackets with a wood chisel. (see the technique on page 33).

STEP 6 Now the pieces are ready for finishing. Make sure that the shelves fit in the cutouts, and cut away any material on the brackets with a wood chisel if they are too tight. It's better that they be rather tight, so the construction will be more stable. If there is a little gap, you can fix it when you glue the shelves later in STEP 12.

STEP 7 To strengthen the construction, you should place a screw through the cutouts in the shelf from the back of the brackets. Pre-bore the holes in the brackets so they won't split when you screw: Use a ⅛-inch (3mm) bore centered on the cutouts, so the holes will be centered on the shelf. Countersink the holes on the back of the brackets, so the screwheads won't be visible when they are screwed in.

STEP 8 In order to hang the shelves on the wall, you'll use two hanger plates (keyhole fittings), one on each shelf holder. Place the fitting centered on the back of the brackets, 6 inches (150 mm) down from the top edge; trace the outer contours of the fitting.

STEP 9 Now you'll countersink the fitting (see technique on page 37), so it won't stick up above the wood. Use a 9⁄16-inch (14mm) bore and bore in line with your outline. Bore down only about 5⁄64 inch (2 mm), just enough so the fitting is sunken. Use a wood chisel to cut away any material left inside your markings.

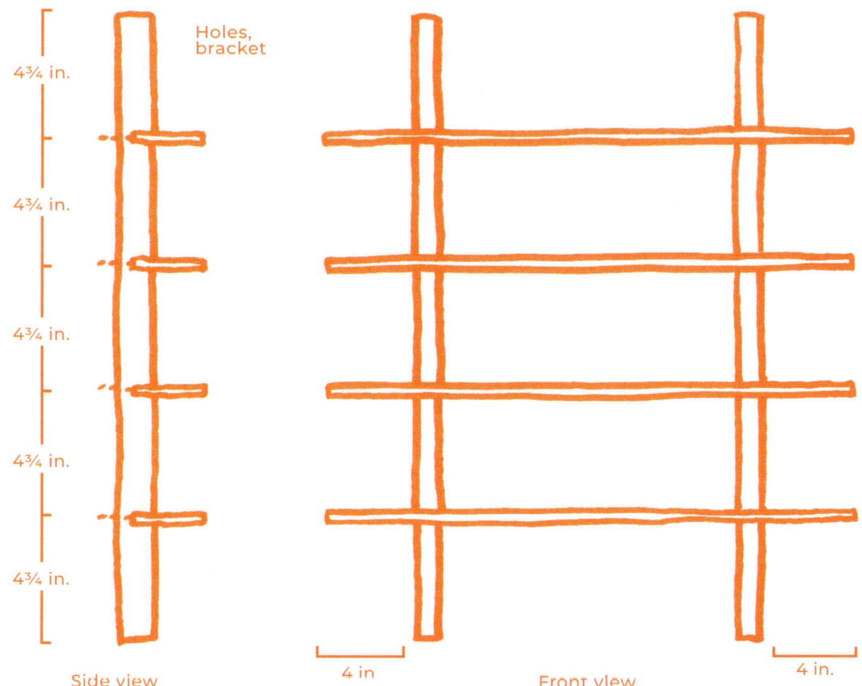

STEP 10 Lay the fitting in its hole and trace the "keyhole." Keep in mind that the narrow part of the keyhole will be upward. Remove the fitting and then bore two holes with a ⅜-inch (10mm) bore, one over the other in each keyhole marking. The hole should be about ¼ inches (6 mm) deep. Chisel away any material between the hole so you'll have an elongated hole. Then, screw the fitting securely into the brackets with $\frac{3}{32}$-by-¾-inch (2.5 × 20 mm) screws.

STEP 11 Lightly sand the shelves and brackets with 240-grit sandpaper. Break the edges and corners with sandpaper. You can break the edges as much or as little as you like; it's totally up to your own taste.

STEP 12 Now it's time to glue the rack together. Make small marks on the shelves where they meet the brackets, so you'll know that they are placed correctly and will stick out to the same width on both sides when you glue.

Begin gluing at the top and bottom shelves: spread the glue on the cutouts and then set the shelves in place so they sit well. If it's tricky to fit them in, use a clamp or tap in with a mallet. In that case, place a block or piece of leather in between to avoid marking the wood. If it's the opposite problem and the cutouts are too big, you can poke shavings in beneath the shelves to tighten them. You can cut shavings from a bit of waste wood or use shavings from the bracket cut-

outs. In this case, do the preparations before you glue. Make sure that the shavings have glue on both sides.

Once you've fitted in the first two shelves, turn the shelf so you can screw in $\frac{9}{64}$-by-1$\frac{9}{16}$-inch (3.5 × 40mm) screws from the back of the brackets into the shelves. After you've screwed them in, use a try square to check that the shelves and brackets are at 90° angles to each other. Wipe away any excess glue with a damp rag. Let it dry for about 20 minutes and then glue in the other two shelves the same way.

STEP 13 Once the glue has dried completely (about 30 minutes), you can cut away any excess glue with a chisel. Do the same if you poked shavings in when gluing—chip away anything that

sticks out, using a wood chisel. Then, use 240-grit sandpaper to sand around the surfaces that were glued. If you feel satisfied, you can now oil the rack.

STEP 14 Use a brush or sponge to spread a layer of boiled linseed oil. Do not oil the back of the brackets because that can leave oil flecks on the wall. Leave to dry about 20 minutes and then wipe off any excess oil. Repeat the day after and let dry before you hang the rack on the wall.

CUTTING BOARD

Cutting boards come in all possible shapes and materials, such as glass, plastic, and laminated, but clearly the best feeling is a wooden cutting board. A nice cutting board is an important detail for a kitchen. My favorite is an old classic board with two horse heads as a handle. I designed and made a somewhat more modern variation of it.

TOOLS
4 clamps
4 tensioning boards for gluing
Japanese saw
Folding rule
Sandpaper, 120, 180, and 240
Sanding block
Jack or bench plane
Wood chisel
Chip-carving knife or hook knife
Carving knife
Coping saw
Half-round file
Carbon paper
Try square
Wood bore ⅜ and 13⁄64 in. (10 and 5mm)
Sponge and rag

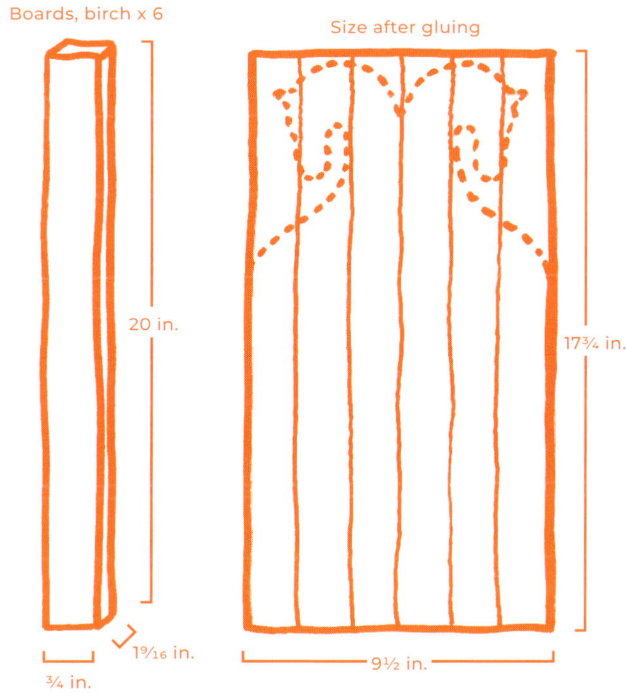

MATERIALS
6 × 20 in. (3 m) planed birch, ¾ × 1 9⁄16 in. (20 × 40mm)
Boiled linseed oil
Wood glue for exterior use

STEP 1 Measure and cut the materials, following the illustration on the previous page. Use the Japanese saw.

STEP 2 Glue the battens together in the direction of the annual rings (see drawing below). See page 57 for more on how to do this. Try to make as little difference in the level as possible with the wood joins, because you probably won't have access to a machine plane, so you'll have to even out any differences in the levels by hand.

STEP 3 Make a clean cut on one end of the cutting board for a straight finish. Draw a line, using a try square about ⅜ inch (10 mm) from the uneven edge. It'll be easier to cut if there is material on both sides of the saw. Use a Japanese saw. See page 25 for help on sawing straight. File and sand the edge until it's fine. If you have a bench plane, you can use it.

STEP 4 Cut away any glue residue with a wood chisel. Then, use a plane to even out any differences in level along the glued joins (see how to plane glued joins on page 29). If you don't have a plane, you can sand off the unevenness. In that case, use a sanding block and begin with 120-grit sandpaper. Change to finer paper afterwards. If you have a machine sander, you can use it with the same grit of paper as above. If you used a plane, you can finish by sanding with 240-grit sandpaper.

STEP 5 Trace a template of the horse heads or draw your own version. When you're satisfied with your template, lay the carbon paper on the cutting board, with the carbon facing down. Lay the motif on top of the carbon paper and draw the lines so the motif will be copied onto the cutting board. If you don't have any carbon paper, you can trace the motif, cut it out, and then draw the contours onto the cutting board.

STEP 6 Use a ⅜-inch (10mm) bore to bore the neck rounding on the horse heads, so the rounding will be perfect. It can be difficult to do this well with only a saw. Do the same using a 13/64-inch (5mm) bore to round the back necks where the two horse heads meet. Make sure you have a block or board against the back so it won't fan out when you bore through.

STEP 7 Tension the cutting board into a bench with the horse heads free in the air. Cut out the shape, using a coping saw, close to the lines you drew. Finesse with a rasp, file, and sandpaper until you're happy with the edges.

STEP 8 Tension the piece so the entire cutting board lies flat on the work surface. Carve out the contours of the back neck, mane, and eyes with a

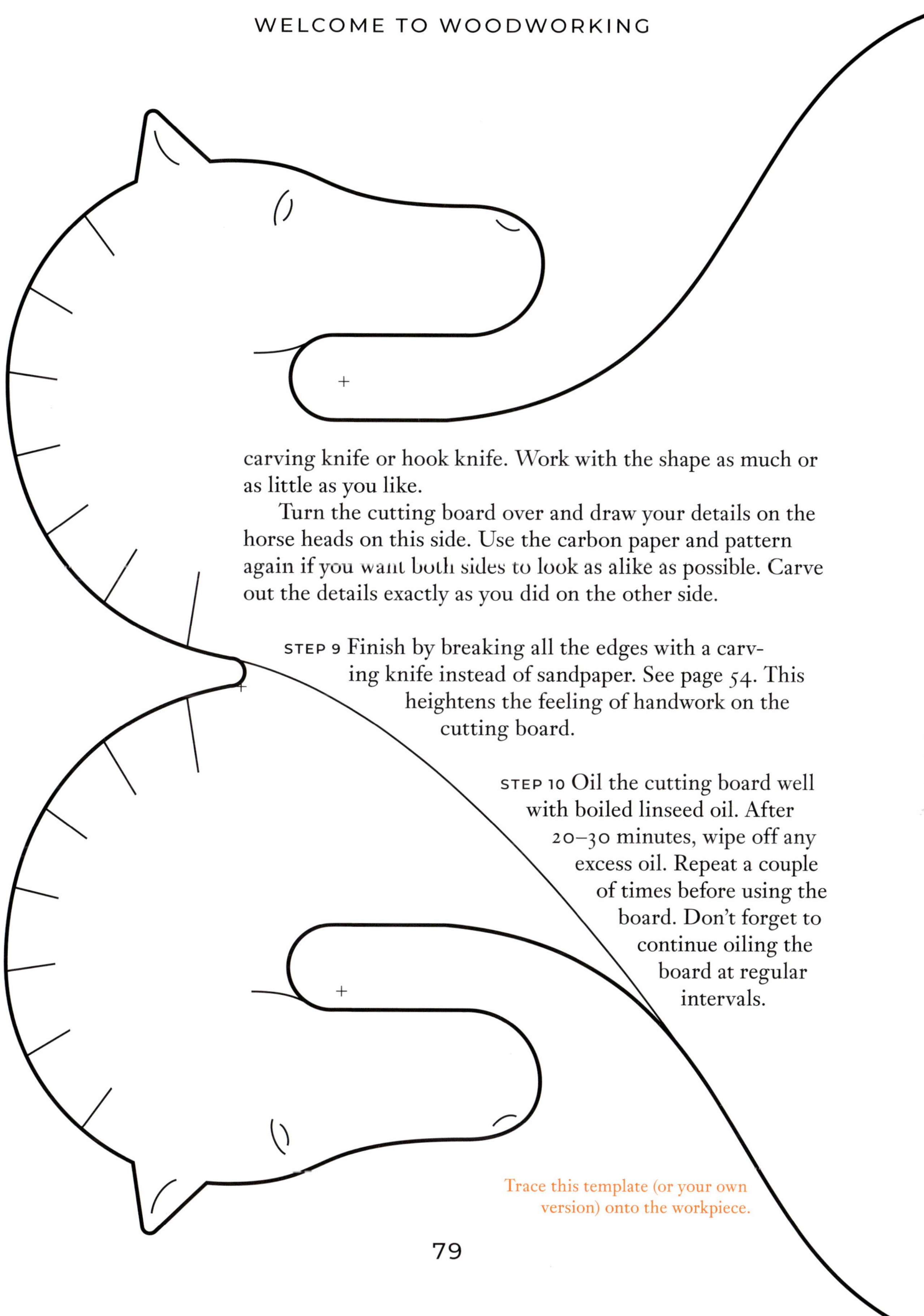

carving knife or hook knife. Work with the shape as much or as little as you like.

Turn the cutting board over and draw your details on the horse heads on this side. Use the carbon paper and pattern again if you want both sides to look as alike as possible. Carve out the details exactly as you did on the other side.

STEP 9 Finish by breaking all the edges with a carving knife instead of sandpaper. See page 54. This heightens the feeling of handwork on the cutting board.

STEP 10 Oil the cutting board well with boiled linseed oil. After 20–30 minutes, wipe off any excess oil. Repeat a couple of times before using the board. Don't forget to continue oiling the board at regular intervals.

Trace this template (or your own version) onto the workpiece.

HERB-DRYING RACK

Anyone growing plants on their balcony or in a garden knows that herbs can sometimes multiply so much that it becomes hard to eat everything when it's fresh. So, the perfect solution is to obtain a rack where you can spread out and hang herbs and then later hang it up on a hook in the ceiling.

You can also use the rack for drying mushrooms and avoid having to dry them on a bench or floor. Because heat rises, the mushrooms or herbs will dry even faster when the rack hangs at the ceiling!

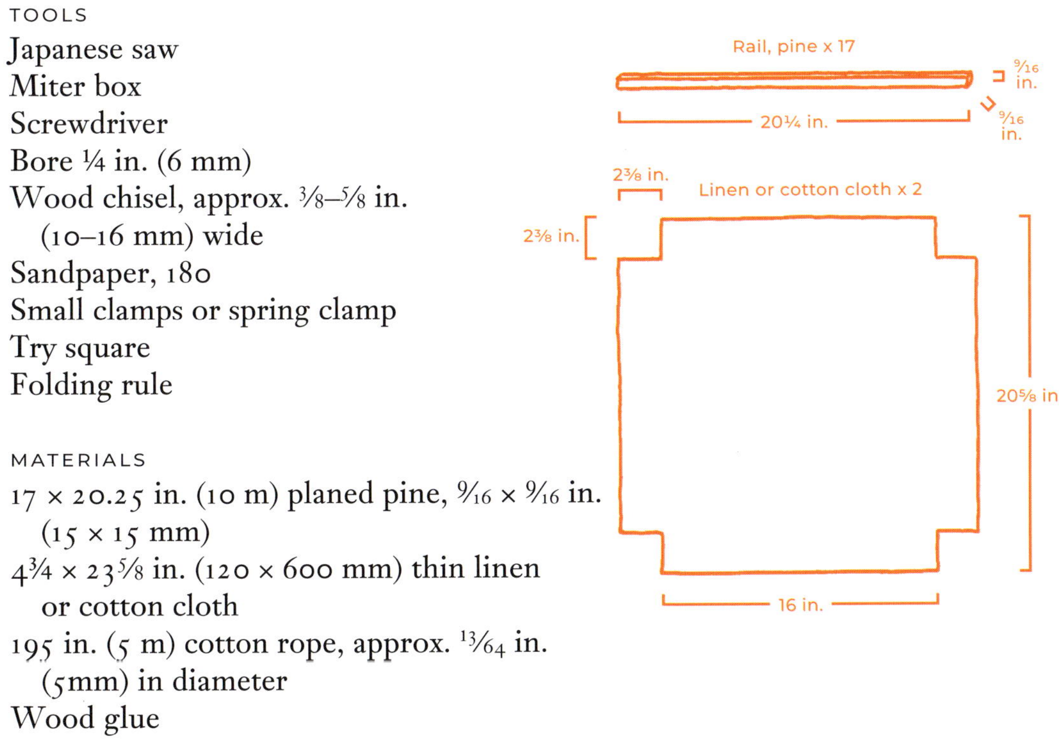

TOOLS

Japanese saw
Miter box
Screwdriver
Bore ¼ in. (6 mm)
Wood chisel, approx. ⅜–⅝ in. (10–16 mm) wide
Sandpaper, 180
Small clamps or spring clamp
Try square
Folding rule

MATERIALS

17 × 20.25 in. (10 m) planed pine, 9⁄16 × 9⁄16 in. (15 × 15 mm)
4¾ × 23⅝ in. (120 × 600 mm) thin linen or cotton cloth
195 in. (5 m) cotton rope, approx. 13⁄64 in. (5mm) in diameter
Wood glue

STEP 1 Measure and cut the materials following the illustrations on the previous page. Use a miter box and Japanese saw.

STEP 2 All the pieces for the three frames will be joined by lap joints (see technique on page 31). The bottom frame has five crossbars instead of being covered with fabric as for the top two. Mark the rails where you'll cut. See the measurements on the drawing. Follow the instructions for a lap joint, cross, on page 33. Cut following the drawing below on all 17 rails.

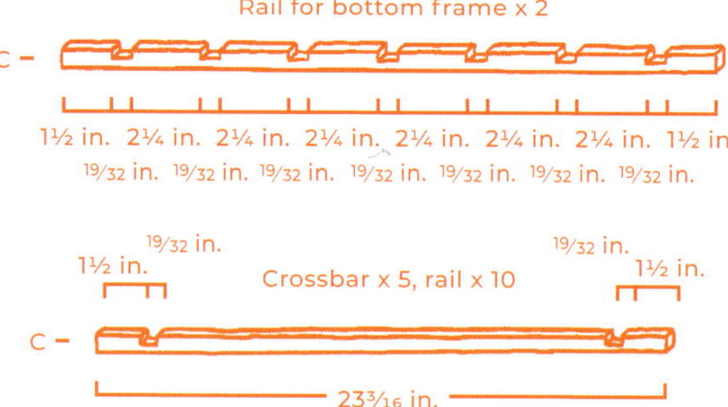

STEP 3 Now glue the frames. Begin by assembling all the frames without glue, to make sure they will fit. Chisel away a little more material if they are too tight or too shallow in some places, until all the pieces fit well.

Once everything fits, you can begin gluing. Begin with one corner, making sure that all the contact surfaces have glue on them. Tension with a small clamp or place in a spring clamp. Use a try square to ensure that all the pieces lie at a 90° angle. If you have enough clamps, you can put the whole frame together all at the same time—just make sure that all the corners are at 90°. If you only have one clamp, you'll have to wait until the glue sets (at least 10 minutes) before you remove the clamp and can continue to the next corner. Wipe off any excess glue with a damp rag before the glue dries.

When the frames are glued together, you can then glue the crossbars for the bottom frame. Work as described above.

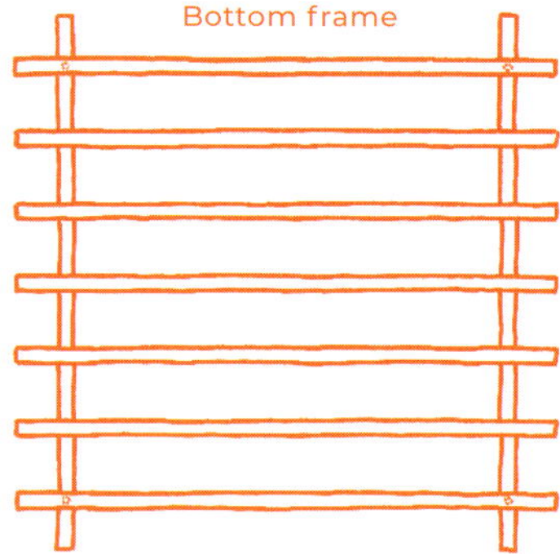

STEP 4 Bore holes at the center of each corner with a ¼-inch (6mm) bore. See drawing below.

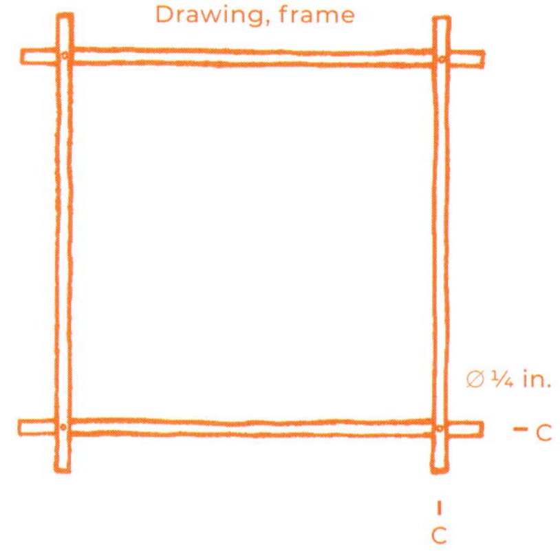

STEP 5 Sand the frames with 180-grit sandpaper. You don't need to be too careful here; just break the edges a little and sand the joints to remove any unevenness.

STEP 6 Now the fabric can be glued to frames 1 and 2. I chose a thin, loosely woven linen fabric for good air circulation.

Cut out the fabric, following the measurements on the drawing on page 81.

Lay the fabric out on a flat surface and spread a thin layer of glue on one side of the frame, where the fabric will be attached. Let the glue dry a bit—it should be sticky rather than wet. Lay the frame on the fabric, lightly pressing it down with your hand so the whole frame is in contact with the fabric. Glue the edges securely around the frame so it's covered by the fabric. Repeat with the second frame.

Assembly of fabric

STEP 7 Cut the rope into 4 equal pieces. Make a knot at one end of each of the four pieces and draw through the batten frame. Make four new knots

6 inches (150 mm) in from the first, and draw it through one of the cloth-covered frames; then do the same again for the last frame. Knot all four ends together to desired length. Make sure that all four rope pieces are the same length to the knot; otherwise, the rack will hang crookedly. Hang the rack directly to the top knot. The herb rack does not need any surface finishing.

BEDSIDE LAMP

I made a bedside lamp that was well fitted to my headboard shown on page 95, but it would also be fine attached directly on the wall.

The construction is simple and based on a fine little hanging armature. When you craft this lamp, it's important to measure correctly for a good result.

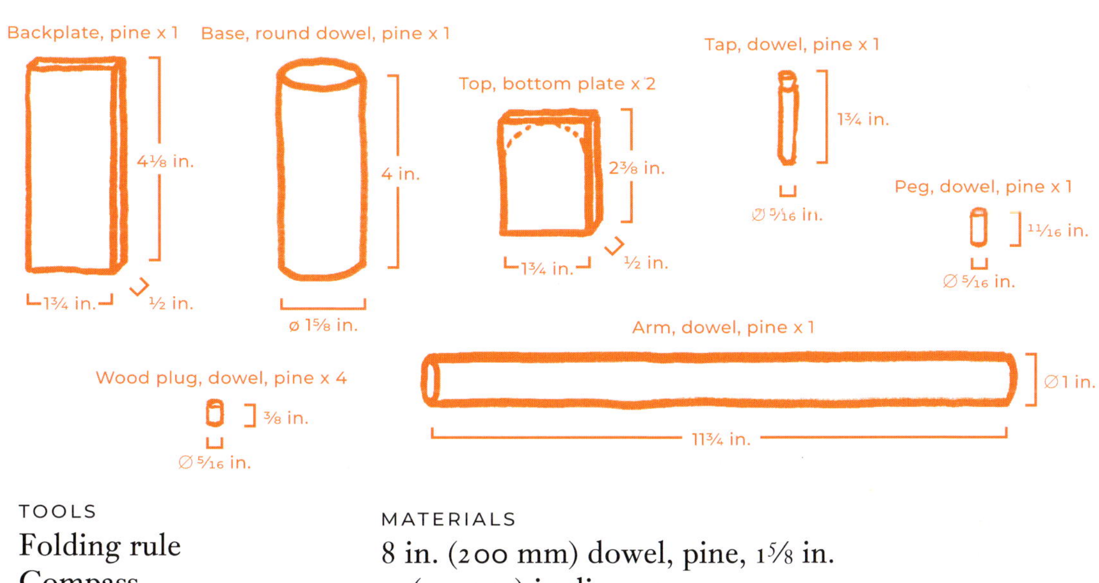

TOOLS

Folding rule
Compass
Auger bore 1 in. (25 mm)
Bore 5⁄64, ⅛, 15⁄64, 5⁄16 in. (2, 3, 6, and 8 mm)
Clamp
Carving knife
Miter box
Japanese saw
Try square
Coping saw
Sandpaper, 150 and 240
Rubber mallet

MATERIALS

8 in. (200 mm) dowel, pine, 1⅝ in. (43 mm) in diameter
19¾ in. (500 mm) dowel, pine, 1 in. (25 mm) in diameter
8 in. (200 mm) dowel, pine, 5⁄16 in. (8 mm) in diameter
19¾ in. (500 mm) planed pine, ½ × 1¾ in. (12 × 45 mm)
4 screws with countersunk heads, 9⁄64 × 1 in. (3.5 × 25 mm)
2 screws with round heads 3⁄16 × 2⅜ in. (4.5 × 60 mm)
2 screws with countersunk heads, 5⁄32 × 1½ in. (4 × 40 mm) (for attaching to wall)

STEP 1 Measure and cut all the materials, following the drawings on the previous page. The lamp consists of a wall hanger (made with a top piece, bottom piece, and backplate), a movable base, and a lamp arm. Cut all the pieces for the lamp except for the base. Use the miter box and Japanese saw and be very careful with all the cuts. It's important that all the measurements match in millimeters.

STEP 2 The base is made with a dowel 1⅝ inches (43mm) in diameter. In order to bore the hole for the lamp arm into the base, you must first secure it firmly, which can be a little problematic due to the round shape. So, work as follows: Bore two holes with a ¼-inch (6mm) bore through the dowel that will be the base, about ¾ inches (20 mm) in from each end. Then, screw it securely with two roundhead screws 2⅜ inches (60 mm) straight down into the pieces or down into one sheet/board that you don't care about and that can be secured as an underlayer. This stabilizes the dowel and allows you to bore the large hole in a good way.

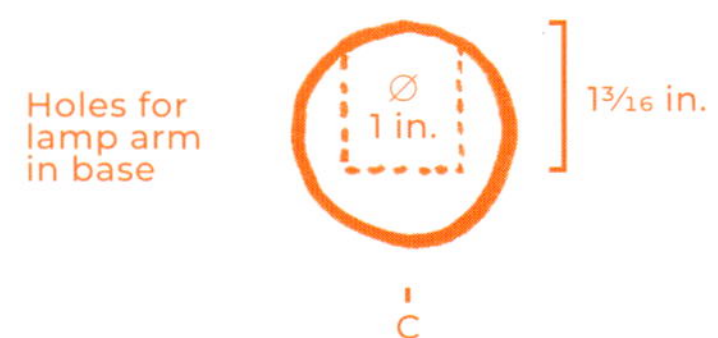

STEP 3 Mark the center of the base and, at the same time, be sure to make the markings where it should be cut on each respective end (see measurements on drawing). Bore with a 1-inch (25mm) auger bore. Bore as vertically as possible! Be careful when you bore these holes—you want to go down as far as possible without going through. You can bore about 1³⁄₁₆ inches (30 mm) down in the dowel. It's better to stop and measure the hole one time too many!

STEP 4 After you've bored the hole, you can loosen the base from the underlay and cut it to the correct length. Use a miter box for a straighter cut.

STEP 5 Sand the cut edges of the base with 150-grit sandpaper and a sanding block. Lightly break the edges with 240-grit sandpaper.

STEP 6 Secure the base and bore a hole at the center of both ends with a ⁵⁄₁₆-inch (8mm) bore. See the illustration below for the depth.

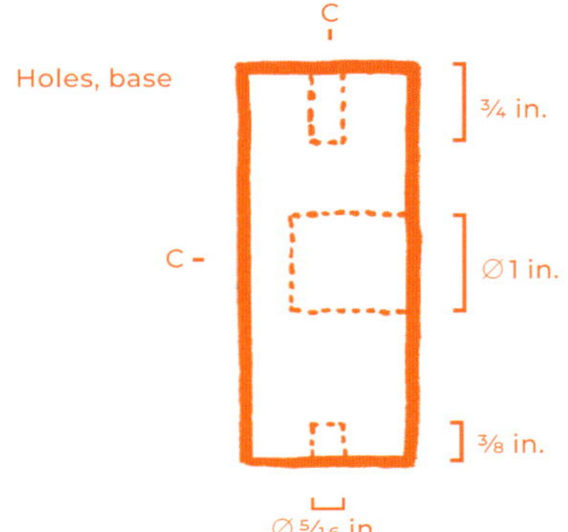

STEP 7 Glue the ¹¹⁄₁₆-inch (17mm) long peg into the hole, which is ⅜ inch (10 mm) deep. This is the underside of the base. Wipe away any excess glue with a

damp rag. Lightly smooth the edges of the tap with 240-grit sandpaper.

STEP 8 You can carve a little neck on one end of the peg for the topside of the base so it'll be a little easier to grip. Bevel the edge of the other end (see photo on page 89).

STEP 9 Bore holes for the cord in the lamp arm with a ¼-inch (6mm) bore (see measurements on drawing). The holes should be absolutely parallel to each other.

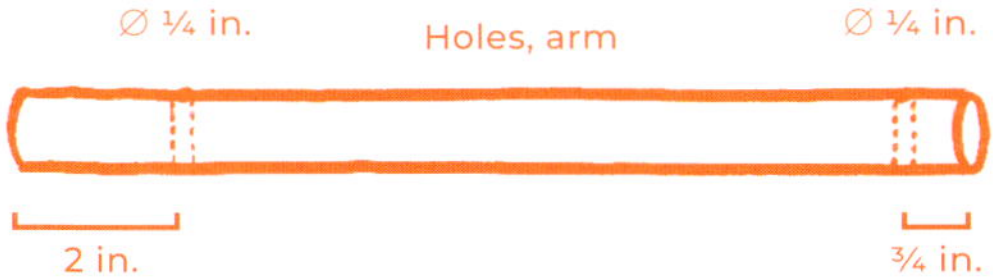

STEP 10 Sand the cut surface on the side of the arm that will be visible. Break the edge.

The end that will be glued into the base does not need to be sanded, but it should be beveled with either a carving knife, file, or coarser sandpaper. This is to allow any excess glue in the hole to have someplace to go when you glue it.

STEP 11 Glue the arm securely into the base. Make sure that the dowel goes down into the bottom of the hole; tap with a rubber mallet if necessary. Make sure that the hole in the arm is parallel to the base. Wipe away any extra glue with a damp rag.

STEP 12 Now you're finished with the arm, and it's time to make the holder, which will be attached to the wall.

Use a compass to draw a half circle 1¾ inches (45 mm) in diameter on one end of the top piece, and a similar half circle on the bottom piece. Make sure that the half circles reach all the way out to the edges (see illustration on next page).

STEP 13 Bore a hole with a 5⁄16-inch (8mm) bore in the mark the compass left at the center of the marked half circles. On the top piece, bore all the way through, but, on the bottom piece, bore down only ⅛ inch (3 mm). Work carefully!

STEP 14 Cut the rounding on the pieces with a coping saw. File and sand the edges.

STEP 15 The pieces for the wall holder will be screwed and glued together, and then the screws will be covered by a wooden plug that you made with the 5⁄16-inch (8mm) dowel: Mark two holes in the top and bottom pieces (see measurements on drawing on next page). First bore with the 5⁄16-inch (8mm) bit down to half of the wooden piece. Then, bore though with the ⅛-inch (3mm) bit.

STEP 16 Bore two holes in the backplate with a 13⁄64-inch (5mm) bore and countersink the hole (see measurements on drawing).

STEP 17 Place the top and bottom pieces against the backplate so they sit together. Draw the boring holes so the marks are on the backplate's end wood, where the screws will sit. Bore with a 5⁄64-inch (2mm) bore on the marks on the backplate. Glue and screw the top and bottom pieces securely onto the backplate with 9⁄64-by-1-inch (3.5 × 25mm) screws.

STEP 18 Glue the wooden plugs into the holes over the screwheads. Trim the plugs with the Japanese saw or flush saw. Sand the surface even.

STEP 19 Make sure that all the pieces fit together well. If the pegs on the underside are too long, the lamp arm won't fit into the wall holder. In that case, sand or file them down until they fit. Sand off the pieces with 240-grit sandpaper and break the edges. Finish with your choice of oil.

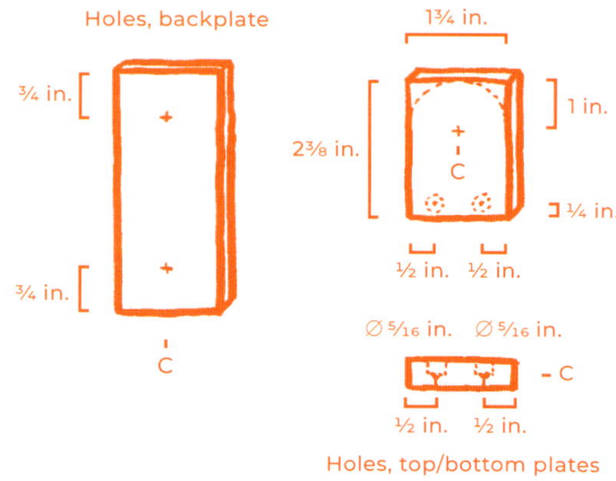

STEP 20 Draw the cord to the lamp through the arm and screw on a lamp base or armature.

STEP 21 Now all the pieces for the lamp are finished. To assemble the lamp, set the arm into the wall piece so the little peg in the bottom on the base clicks into the bored 5⁄16-inch (8mm) hole in the bottom plate on the wall holder. So that the construction locks, you need to loosen the peg that is 1¾ inches (45 mm) long and insert it through the hole on the topside of the base. When you're going to attach the lamp to the wall, if the arm cannot be mounted there, you should first unscrew the wall holder and then set the arm in.

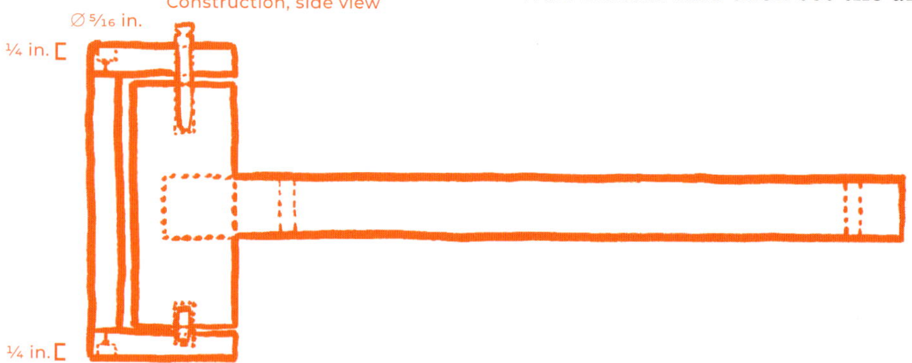

The Ikebana & Bonsai
1979
Daily Record of Engagements

SMALL WALL SHELF

This is a simple little wall shelf that I use for plants because my windowsills simply aren't wide enough. This shelf fits the bill, and it's also great for other items that you'd like to have a special place for on the wall. You can make it as small as you like as long as you follow the construction instructions and keep to about the same measurements I provide.

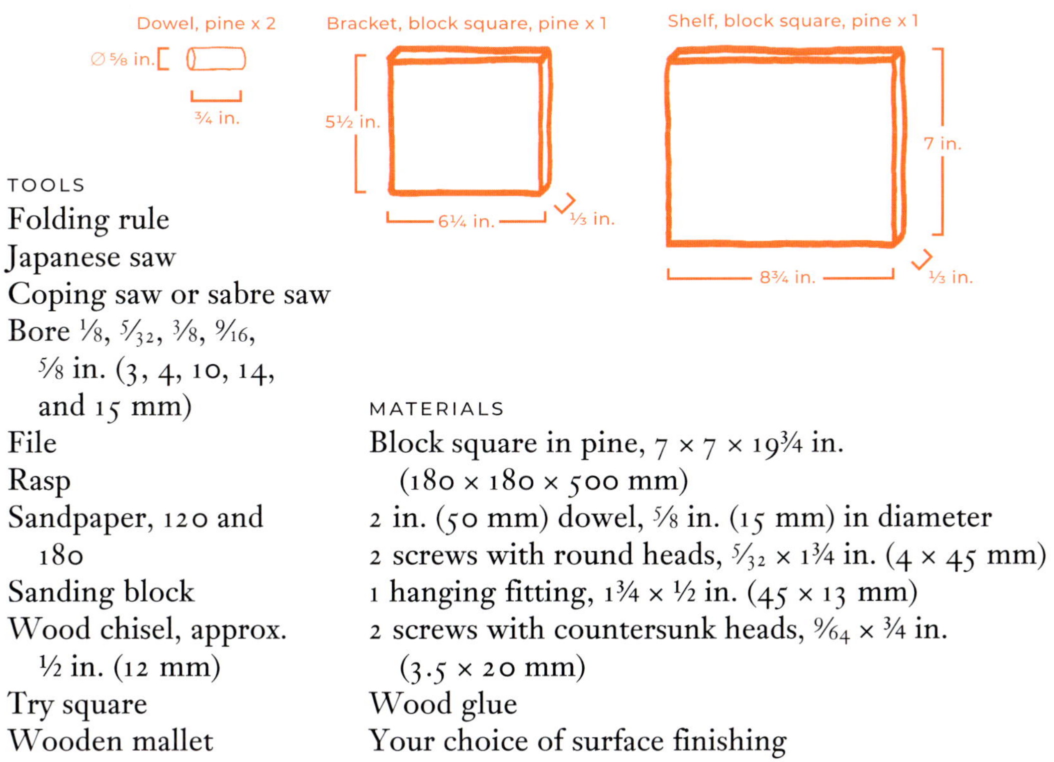

TOOLS

Folding rule
Japanese saw
Coping saw or sabre saw
Bore 1/8, 5/32, 3/8, 9/16, 5/8 in. (3, 4, 10, 14, and 15 mm)
File
Rasp
Sandpaper, 120 and 180
Sanding block
Wood chisel, approx. ½ in. (12 mm)
Try square
Wooden mallet

MATERIALS

Block square in pine, 7 × 7 × 19¾ in. (180 × 180 × 500 mm)
2 in. (50 mm) dowel, 5/8 in. (15 mm) in diameter
2 screws with round heads, 5/32 × 1¾ in. (4 × 45 mm)
1 hanging fitting, 1¾ × ½ in. (45 × 13 mm)
2 screws with countersunk heads, 9/64 × ¾ in. (3.5 × 20 mm)
Wood glue
Your choice of surface finishing

STEP 1 Measure and cut the materials, following the drawings on the previous page. If you want a rectangular shelf, use a try square to draw the lines, and use a Japanese saw and support block so you can cut straight. If you want another shape for the shelf, make it, but don't forget that the side against the wall must be straight so the construction will be stable. If you choose a shape without straight cuts, use a coping saw. Refine the saw cuts with a rasp, file, and sandpaper.

STEP 2 Trace the bracket onto the sheet of pine wood. If it has a corner that is already 90°, you can work out from it; otherwise, begin by sawing a straight cut with a 90° angle to go out from (see measurements on the drawing). Make the shape that you want between the two markings, so you can see what the support should look like. The same recommendations for cutting as above apply here. Refine the saw cuts with a rasp, file, and sandpaper.

STEP 3 Measure to the center of the top of the shelf where the bracket will be attached (see drawing on next page for measurements). Bore down to half the thickness of the sheet wood with a ⅝-inch (15mm) bore on the two markings and then bore the last bit with a 5⁄32-inch (4mm) bore. Next, place the bracket against the bottom of the shelf as it will sit, and bore with a ⅛-inch (3mm) bit down into the bracket through the bored hole in the shelf.

Suggestions for various shapes of the shelf and bracket

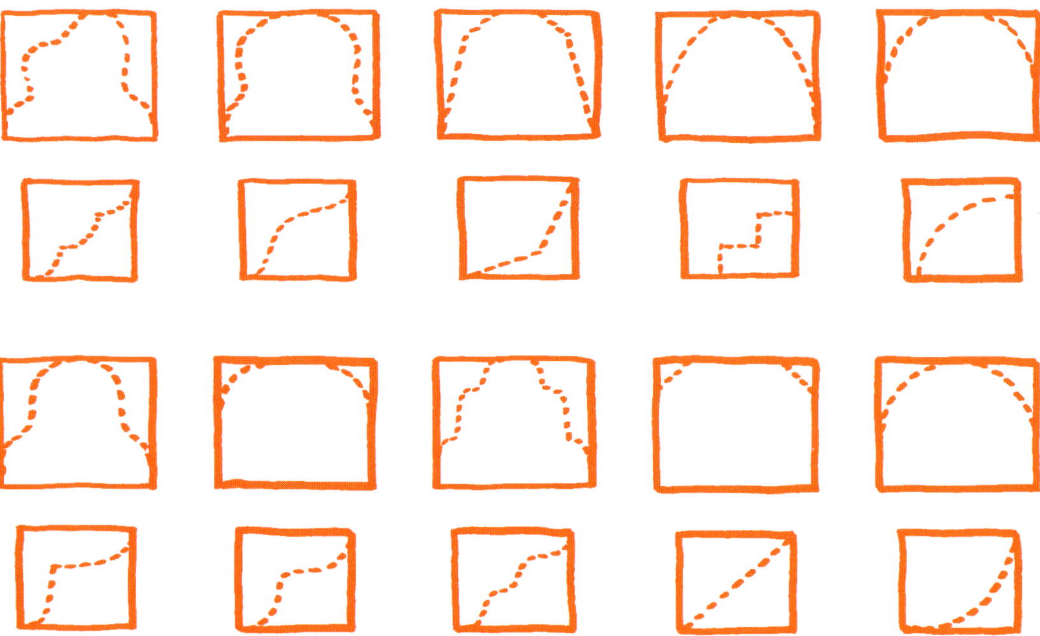

STEP 4 Glue and screw the bracket and shelf together with the 5⁄32-by-1¾-inch (4 × 45mm) screws. Then, glue the wood plugs into the holes. Tap in with a wooden mallet and then wipe away any excess glue with a damp rag.

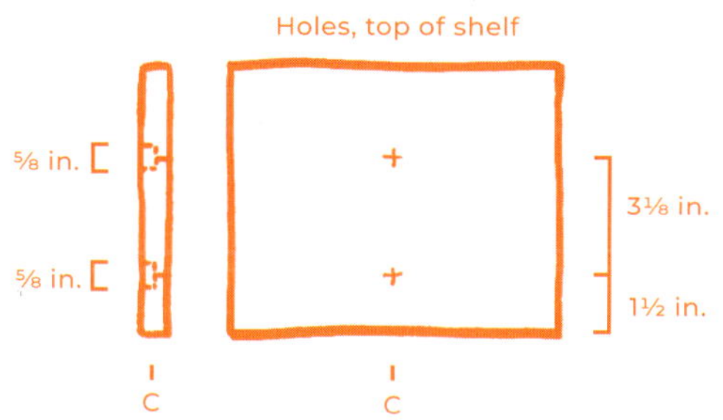

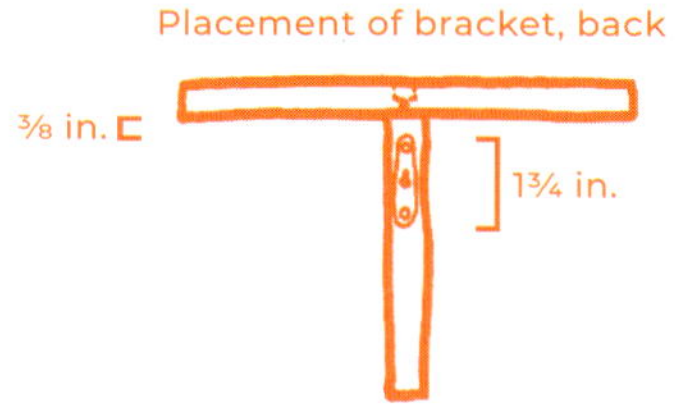

STEP 5 Trace where the hanging fitting will be on the back of the bracket (see drawing for measurements). Attach fitting, following technique on page 37.

STEP 6 When the glue has dried, trim the dowel with the Japanese or flush saw. Sand the surface so it'll be fine and even, using a sanding block. Sand and shape the edges on the shelf as you like.

STEP 7 Finish the surface as you want. I used white-pigmented hard wax oil for my shelves.

HEADBOARD

A headboard can really raise the coziness factor in a bedroom. It makes the bed feel more like a piece of furniture, and I can't imagine a better feeling than waking up with my head all warm and cozy from the wood.

The width of the headboard depends on the width of your bed. This one is designed to fit a bed 86 inches (218 cm) wide. You can choose birch plywood instead of pine plywood if you like that better.

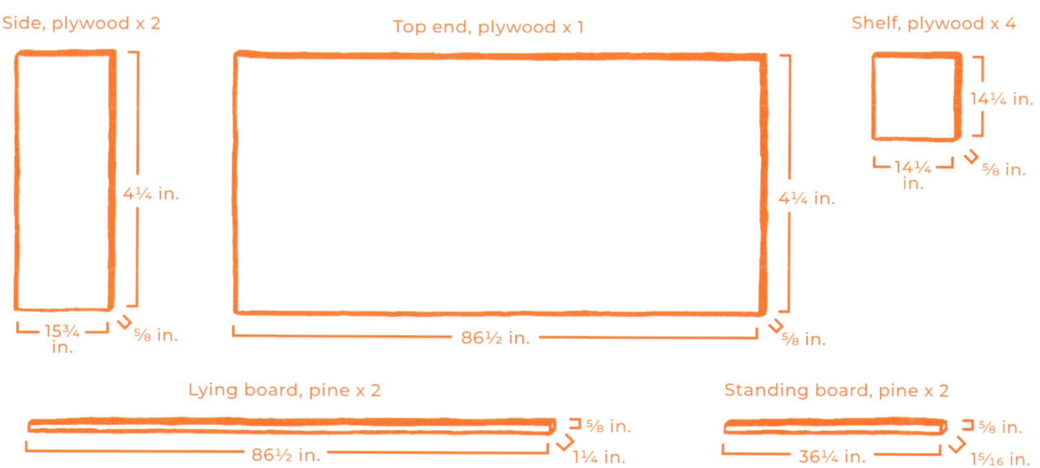

TOOLS
Folding rule
Screwdriver and bits
Bore 9⁄64 in. (3.5 mm) and 5⁄32 in. (4 mm)
Countersink
Sandpaper, 150 and 240
Sanding block or machine sander
Coping saw
Rag or sponge

MATERIALS
2 sheets of plywood, ⅝ in. (16 mm) thick
2 x 86½ and 2 x 36¼ in. planed wood, pine strips, 9⁄16 in. × 1⁵⁄₁₆ in. (15 × 33 mm)
22 brass screws with round countersunk heads, 5⁄32 × 1½ in. (4 × 40 mm)
12 wood screws with countersunk heads, 5⁄32 × 1½ in. (4 × 40 mm)
25 wood screws with countersunk heads, 9⁄64 × 1 in. (3.5 × 25 mm)
Wood glue
Hard wax oil

STEP 1 Have the pine plywood cut to the correct measurements at the lumberyard (see measurements on drawing on previous page).

STEP 2 The top end of the headboard should be lined up with strips: Screw the planed strips together securely as a frame on the back of the plywood (see measurements on drawing on previous page). Lay the strips edge to edge along the top edge and sides. Make sure that the lower strips are placed high enough to be above the floor strips. So that the screwheads won't be visible on the front, screw them in from the back. Pre-bore into the strips, first with the 5/32-inch (4mm) bore, and then countersink the holes. Next, screw down with the 9/64-by-1-inch (3.5 × 25mm) screws.

STEP 3 Use the coping saw to cut the floor strips in two pieces, which will be the side. Make an accurate template in paper or cardboard, which you can cut out, or cut out the shape on the strips. Lay the template on the plywood, trace it, and then cut, following the lines, and nicely finish it with sandpaper.

STEP 4 Mark where you want to pre-bore the holes for the screws on the side pieces on the top end (measure following the illustration). It's important that they are aligned and spaced evenly because the screws will be visible. Begin with the 5/32-inch (4mm) bore, then use the countersink.

STEP 5 Screw the sides of the top of the headboard: Place the sides edge to edge with the pieces on the back of the top end. Bore first through the previously bored holes with the 9/64-inch (3.5mm) bore and then screw them together with the brass screws. When you screw in the brass screws, make sure you do so very carefully, because they break rather easily since they are so soft.

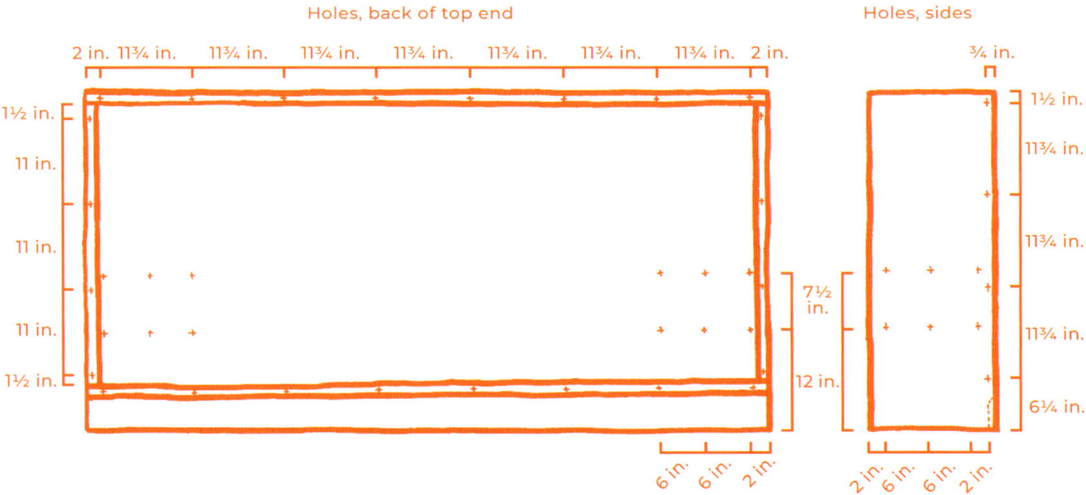

STEP 6 Mark the place on the headboard for the shelves. Mark both sides and the end and in the join where they meet. Make sure that everything is horizontal. The height of the shelves depends on the height of the bed and how much space you want between the two shelves. My shelves are placed relative to the standard bed height. Measure to make sure yours will fit your bed.

STEP 7 Starting at the marks for the shelf placement, make new markings for boring the holes for the screws to attach the shelves. If you marked the placement of the shelves on the top of the shelf, the markings for the holes should be 5⁄16 inch (8 mm) lower so the screw will be in the middle of the shelf. Space the markings following the illustration.

STEP 8 Countersink the holes in the headboard with a 5⁄32-inch (4mm) bore. The screws on the sides will be visible, so bore the holes aligned and evenly spaced. Countersink the hole.

STEP 9 Screw and glue the shelves: Hold the shelf in place and trace the bore holes on the headboard to mark the shelves where the screws will go in. Bore the shelves at the marks with a 9⁄64-inch (3.5mm) bore, so the plywood won't split, which can easily happen when you're screwing into end wood. Apply glue to the ends of each shelf and then screw in each shelf with 5⁄32-by-1½-inch (4 × 40mm) screws with round heads to the sides and 5⁄32-by-1½-inch (4 × 40mm) wood screws with countersunk heads into the top end.

STEP 10 Now all the pieces are joined and it's time for sanding. A machine sander will make the job easier for the large surfaces, but it's fine doing this by hand. Most often, finer quality plywood is already rather smooth and only needs sanding with 240-grit sandpaper. If the sheet is rougher, you can begin with 150 and then switch to 240. Break all the edges. Even if you have a machine sander, you'll get the best results by breaking the edges by hand.

STEP 11 I chose to finish my headboard with hard wax oil, which I think gives plywood a fine depth, but without the greasy surface a pure oil can give. Apply the hard wax oil with a rag or sponge and then wipe away any excess oil. Let the oil dry and then sand the whole headboard once more with 240-grit sandpaper. This is done to sand down any fibers that came up with the first application. Oil the headboard once more, and then you're done!

Kött
Mara Lee
MEMORI TOKYO
Bröd och pizza
Richard Olney
SOUTHERN PROVISIONS
REAL COOKING
NIGELLAS KÖK
Nigel Slater Appetite
JENS LINDER LÅNGKOK
MOMOFUKU
WHERE CHEFS EAT
CHEZ PANISSE COOKING
PAUL BERTOLLI
SAMSUNG
The ESCAPIST
London

TV STAND WITH WHEELS

I think it's great to have a living room where I don't always turn all my attention to the television, but at the same time, I like to have it in front of me when I'm lying on the sofa. The solution is a TV stand with wheels so it can be rolled out and then rolled away when not in use.

The measurements are fitted for a 50-inch TV. If your television is larger or smaller, you can adjust the measurements. In that case, don't forget that you'll need to adjust both depth and length.

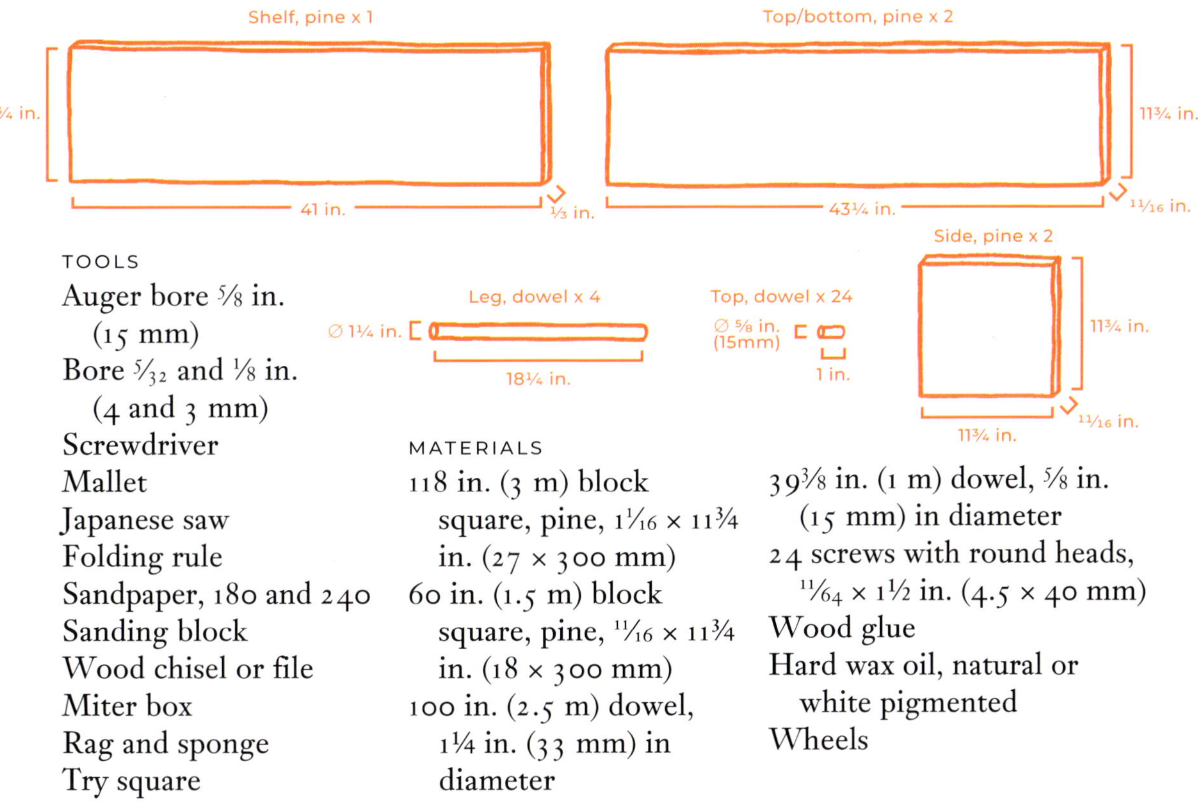

TOOLS

Auger bore ⅝ in. (15 mm)
Bore 5⁄32 and ⅛ in. (4 and 3 mm)
Screwdriver
Mallet
Japanese saw
Folding rule
Sandpaper, 180 and 240
Sanding block
Wood chisel or file
Miter box
Rag and sponge
Try square

MATERIALS

118 in. (3 m) block square, pine, 1 1⁄16 × 11¾ in. (27 × 300 mm)
60 in. (1.5 m) block square, pine, 11⁄16 × 11¾ in. (18 × 300 mm)
100 in. (2.5 m) dowel, 1¼ in. (33 mm) in diameter
39⅜ in. (1 m) dowel, ⅝ in. (15 mm) in diameter
24 screws with round heads, 11⁄64 × 1½ in. (4.5 × 40 mm)
Wood glue
Hard wax oil, natural or white pigmented
Wheels

STEP 1 Have the pine block square cut to the correct measurements at the lumberyard. See measurements in illustration on previous page.

STEP 2 Cut the legs, following measurements in illustration on previous page. Use a miter box and Japanese saw so you'll have straight cuts. Cut at a 90° angle.

STEP 3 Sand the saw cuts with 180-grit sandpaper, using a sanding block.

STEP 4 Mark and bore the holes for joining the top, bottom, and sides (see drawing). Begin by boring with a ⅝-inch (15mm) bore through half the thickness of the wood sheet, about ½ inch (13mm). Then, bore through the whole way with a 5⁄32-inch (4mm) bore.

STEP 5 Bore the holes where the legs will be screwed in (see illustration). Work as in step 4. Begin by boring with a ⅝-inch (15mm) bore and then with a 5⁄32-inch (4mm) bore. Consider boring with the ⅝-inch (15mm) bore on the side that will be inside.

STEP 6 Now you'll assemble all the pieces. Begin with the shelf and sides. Lay out the pieces that will be joined—they form a letter H. The shelf should be centered, so make a mark at the center of the sides and in the middle of the shelf thickness, so you'll know that the shelf is in the right place when the lines meet. Apply glue to the ends of the shelf and screw the pieces together in the countersunk holes. Use a try square to double check that the angles are at 90°.

STEP 7 Set the top and bottom on securely. Spread glue on the ends of the sides and screw in the countersunk holes. You do not need to bore down in the sides. The top/bottom and sides should lie edge to edge. Wipe away any excess glue with a damp rag. You do not need to put a press on these glued pieces because the parts are screwed together. Make sure that the screws are properly screwed in.

STEP 8 Cut the pegs from the ⅝-inch (15mm) diameter dowel (see measurements and amount in drawing below). Smooth one end of the pegs with coarse sandpaper or a knife. Glue the pegs in the hole over the screwheads. Tap in with a wooden or rubber mallet. Wipe away any excess glue with a damp rag.

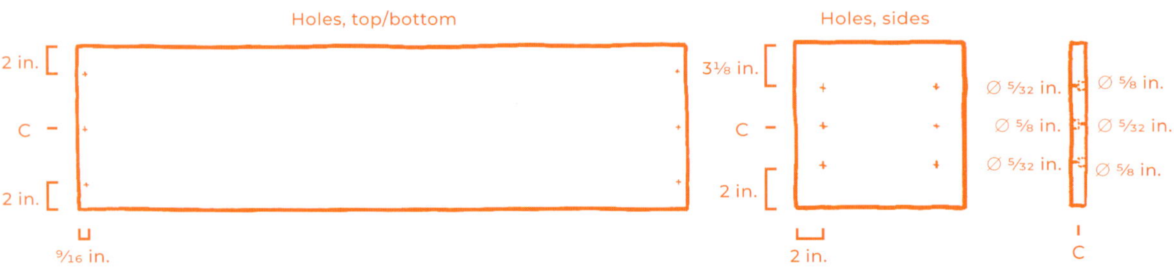

STEP 9 Trim the pegs with a coping saw or flush saw. File or cut away the last bits with a wood chisel and then sand the surface with a sanding block and 180-grit sandpaper.

STEP 10 As necessary, sand down any unevenness at the cuts with 180-grit sandpaper. sand the stand with 240-grit sandpaper. Break the edges and corners, using a sanding block. You should also sand the legs and smooth the edges with 240-grit sandpaper.

STEP 11 Bore a hole at the center of one end of a leg to fit the measurements of the wheels. Press the wheel into the hole.

STEP 12 Now the legs will be screwed into the TV stand. Bore a hole 2 inches (50 mm) from the top edge of the four legs with a ⅛-inch (3mm) bore. Bore about $5/64$ inches (2 mm) in and be careful to bore straight down to the center. Screw the leg into the stand through the top countersunk holes at the sides. Make sure that the leg is parallel and aligned with the stand's sides and then bore through the countersunk hole in the stand into the leg with a ⅛-inch (3mm) bore. Be very careful not to bore through the leg. Next, screw it in securely, precisely as before.

STEP 13 Glue in the rest of the ⅝-inch (15mm) wood plugs into the holes over the screwheads as in step 8.

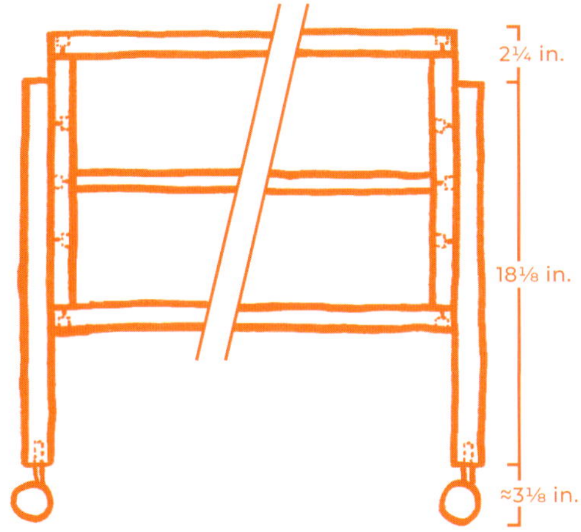

STEP 14 Finish the surface with hard wax oil, applying it with a rag or sponge. Wipe away any excess glue with a damp rag. Let dry and then sand lightly with 240-grit sandpaper. Oil it again as before.

FLOWERPOT STAND

A problem with having a lot of houseplants—a problem I have anyway—is that there are too many plants and too few places to put them. The solution is making a few flowerpot stands! Here's one that is fine and practical with two shelves.

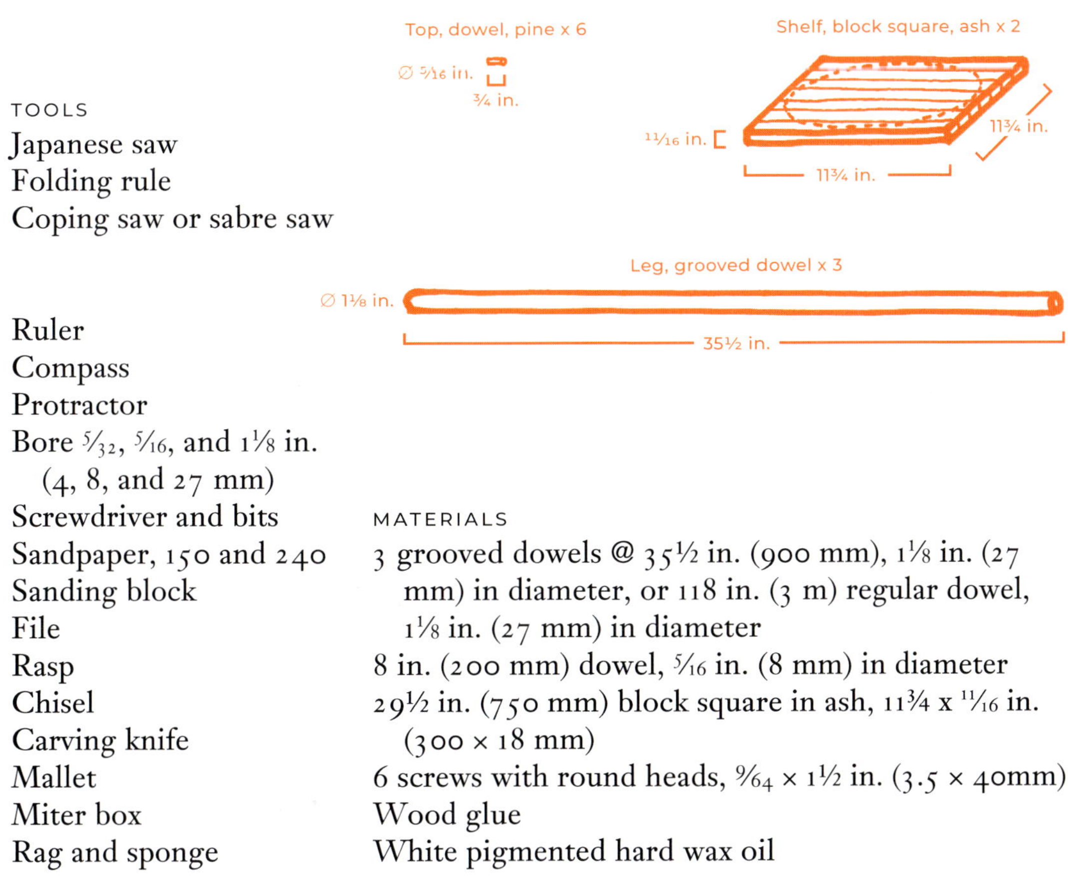

TOOLS

Japanese saw
Folding rule
Coping saw or sabre saw
Ruler
Compass
Protractor
Bore 5/32, 5/16, and 1 1/8 in. (4, 8, and 27 mm)
Screwdriver and bits
Sandpaper, 150 and 240
Sanding block
File
Rasp
Chisel
Carving knife
Mallet
Miter box
Rag and sponge

MATERIALS

3 grooved dowels @ 35 1/2 in. (900 mm), 1 1/8 in. (27 mm) in diameter, or 118 in. (3 m) regular dowel, 1 1/8 in. (27 mm) in diameter
8 in. (200 mm) dowel, 5/16 in. (8 mm) in diameter
29 1/2 in. (750 mm) block square in ash, 11 3/4 x 11/16 in. (300 × 18 mm)
6 screws with round heads, 9/64 × 1 1/2 in. (3.5 × 40mm)
Wood glue
White pigmented hard wax oil

STEP 1 Cut the legs into three pieces, 35½ inches (900 mm) each, if you didn't buy already cut pieces in 35½-inch (900mm) lengths. Use a miter box. Sand the cut surfaces with 150-grit sandpaper and a sanding block. Break the edges. If you want, you can round the ends on the legs for a softer look. See how on page 40.

STEP 2 Bore two holes in each leg with a 5⁄16-inch (8mm) bore. Do not bore all the way through but just about to the middle, about 5⁄8 inches (15 mm). Mark the bore holes as shown in the drawing. Be careful to make the holes parallel with each other. Then, continue to bore in the same hole with a 5⁄32-inch (4mm) bore until you're through the leg.

STEP 3 Draw two circles on the ash sheet, with a diameter of 10¼ inches (260 mm). These pieces will become the shelves. Draw the circles about an inch (a few centimeters) in from the edge of the sheet so you have a little extra material left all around. Use a compass.

STEP 4 Now you can draw where each leg will be on the sheet. Draw lightly with a pencil so it'll be easier to remove the lines later. Begin by drawing a straight line from the center of the circle out to the edge of the circle. This is where the first leg will be placed. Working out from this point, use a protractor to draw out the placements for the second and third legs. Make a mark 120° from the first line and then a line from the center to the mark and again out to the circle. Repeat for the third leg (see drawing below).

Once you've drawn the three lines, you can double-check that there is the same distance between the three points where the lines meet in the drawn circle (see illustration below).

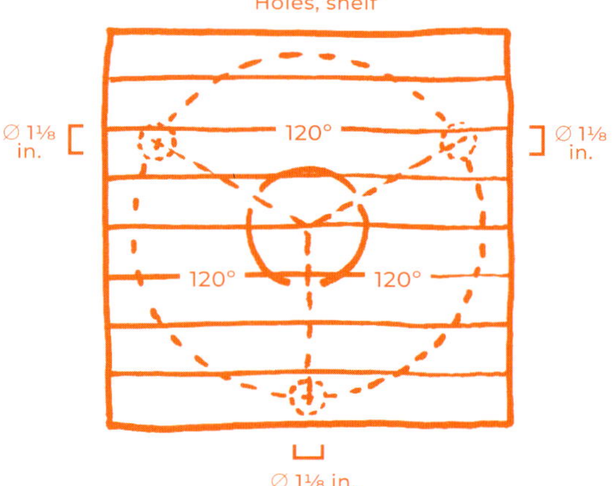

STEP 5 Bore a hole with the 1⅛-inch (27mm) bore at the three points where the lines meet the circle's line. Place the bore bit precisely centered on the line. Do the same on both circles. Bore as straight as you can.

STEP 6 Cut the piece apart, so the two circles are each on one part. Then cut the respective circles, following the line. If you have a sabre saw, you can use it; otherwise, a coping saw is fine.

STEP 7 Rasp, file, and sand the edges until they are fine.

STEP 8 Erase the pencil lines and sand the shelves with 240-grit sandpaper. I chose rounded edges, but just breaking the edges is also nice.

STEP 9 Oil the shelves with the white pigmented hard wax oil. Wipe away any excess oil, lightly sand with 240-grit sandpaper, and then oil once more. Make sure that no oil gets into the half circles where the leg will be attached, or the glue won't stick.

STEP 10 Now securely attach the legs to the shelves. Take one leg at a time. Spread a little glue in the half circle where the leg will be attached. Poke the screw through so the point is visible through the hole in the leg—that way, you can see if the screw is centered on the shelf. Screw it in securely. So the same with all the legs. Wipe off any excess glue with a damp rag.

STEP 11 Cut pegs from the 5⁄16-inch (8mm) dowel (see measurements and numbers in illustration on page 103). Soften the edge on one end of the pegs with coarse sandpaper or a knife. Make sure that the screws are properly screwed in, and then glue the pegs in with the smoothed edge into the hole where the screw is. Make sure that the peg goes all the way in. Tap it with a rubber or wooden mallet if necessary. Wipe off any excess glue with a damp rag. Let dry.

STEP 12 Cut the pegs with a Japanese or sabre saw and then file and sand the rest so the peg fits with the dowel.

STEP 13 I decided to leave the legs on my stand unfinished, and only sanded them with 240-grit sandpaper.

KNIFE HOLDER

I made a freestanding knife holder for storing all my best-quality knives, those I want to see most. The knife holder doesn't hide the knife blade, which I think is the most impressive feature of a fine knife. I decided to use oak, which fits with my kitchen and because it's a dense type of wood that makes the holder more stable. The mortise-and-tenon joints are unbelievably pretty but a little fiddly—if you think it's challenging, you can first try to make a couple in a softer wood, such as pine.

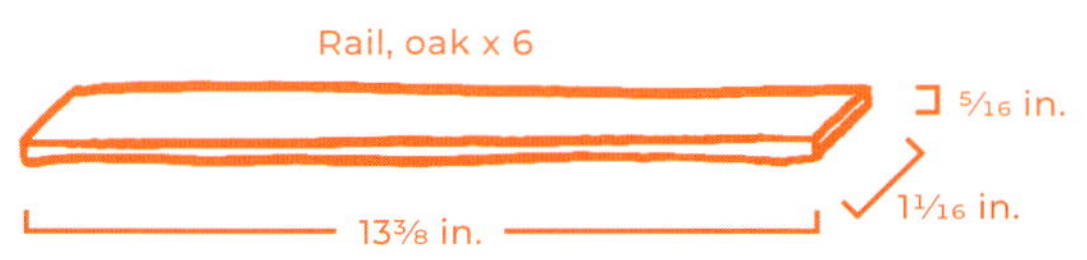

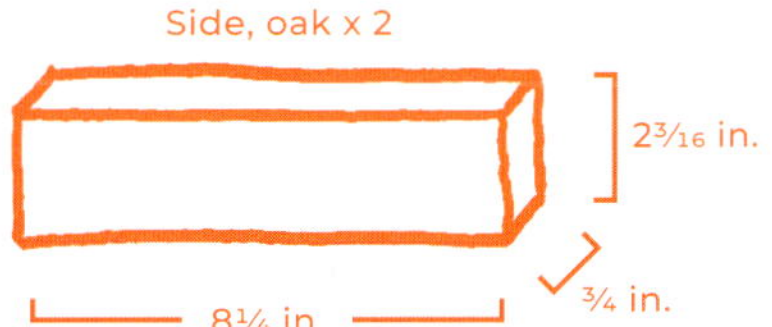

TOOLS

Folding rule
Try square
Japanese saw
6 clamps
Ruler
Wood chisel, 5⁄16 and 3⁄4 in. (8 mm and approx. 20 mm)
Miter box
Rubber or wooden mallet
Sandpaper, 150 and 240
Sanding block
Brush or sponge

MATERIALS

96 in. (2.4 m) planed wood, oak, 5⁄16 × 1 1⁄16 in. (8 × 27 mm)
25 9⁄16 in. (650 mm) planed oak, 3⁄4 × 2 3⁄16 in. (21 × 56 mm)
Wood glue for exterior use
Boiled linseed oil

STEP 1 Begin by cutting the rails, following the illustration on the previous page. Use a miter box so you can cut at a 90° angle. Next, cut the sides somewhat longer than shown in the drawing. Cut them 9½ inches (240 mm) long so you have an extra inch (a couple of centimeters) in case the cut isn't correct and you need to re-do it. Make sure that one end of the pieces is finely cut at a 90° angle. This is the side you'll make the mortise-and-tenon joint with.

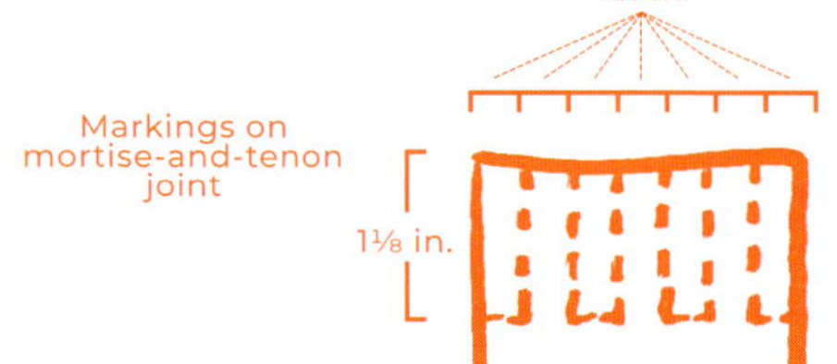

STEP 2 Make a mortise-and-tenon joint on the two sides, using the technique described on page 35. When you've finished them, you can make a finishing cut on the other end of the sides, using the length measurement in the illustration. Be extra careful to make a straight cut at a 90° angle.

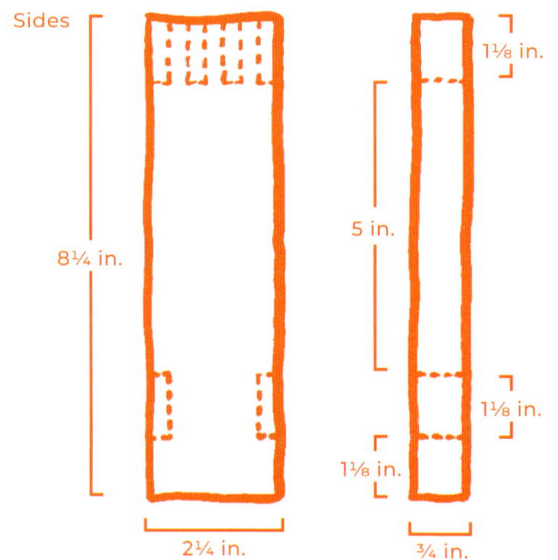

STEP 3 Mark the cut-outs for the two rails that will sit on each side of the knife holder (see measurements on drawing). Lay the slat where it'll be inserted, and make a mark on the bottom and top edge to mark the width. Cut inside your markings the same way as if you were making a crossed lap joint (see technique on page 33).

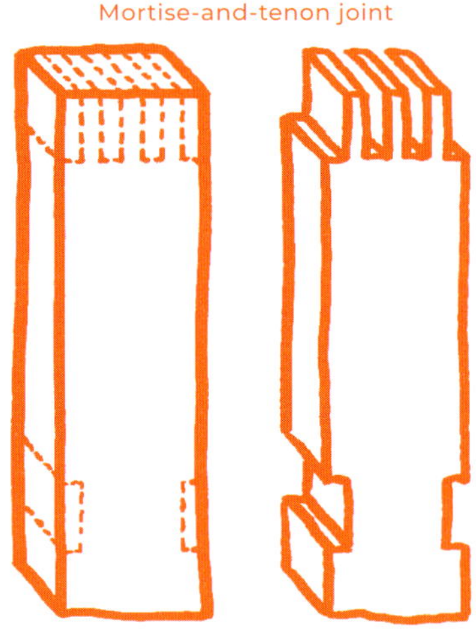

STEP 4 Now it's time to glue. Use an exterior-use wood glue because it's more water resistant. Don't apply too much glue on the surfaces to be glued, because it can be difficult to wipe the excess away between the slats if any squeezes out. Glue all the pieces at the same time, tapping down the slats with a rubber mallet if they are tight. You can use a wooden mallet if you have a block between the wood piece and the mallet, so you won't leave any marks from the mallet on the knife holder. Clamp from the side and, if necessary, from the top. Check with

a try square to make sure the angles are 90°. Wipe away any glue that was pressed out between the slats, with a slightly damp rag.

STEP 5 Once the glue has dried, it's time to sand. Begin with 150-grit sandpaper and sand down any unevenness at the joins. When everything is even, change to 240-grit sandpaper to refine the surface. Break the edges.

STEP 6 Use a brush or sponge to apply the oil. Let dry for about 30 minutes, wipe off any excess oil, and then apply another layer once the first layer is dry.

STOOL

This stool, or small bench, was inspired by my favorite bench "Visingsö," drawn by Carl Malmsten. It's exactly wide enough for two people to sit together and, at the same time, is very versatile and easy to set in place because it's so simple. It looks easy to make, but I consider it one of the hardest projects in this book.

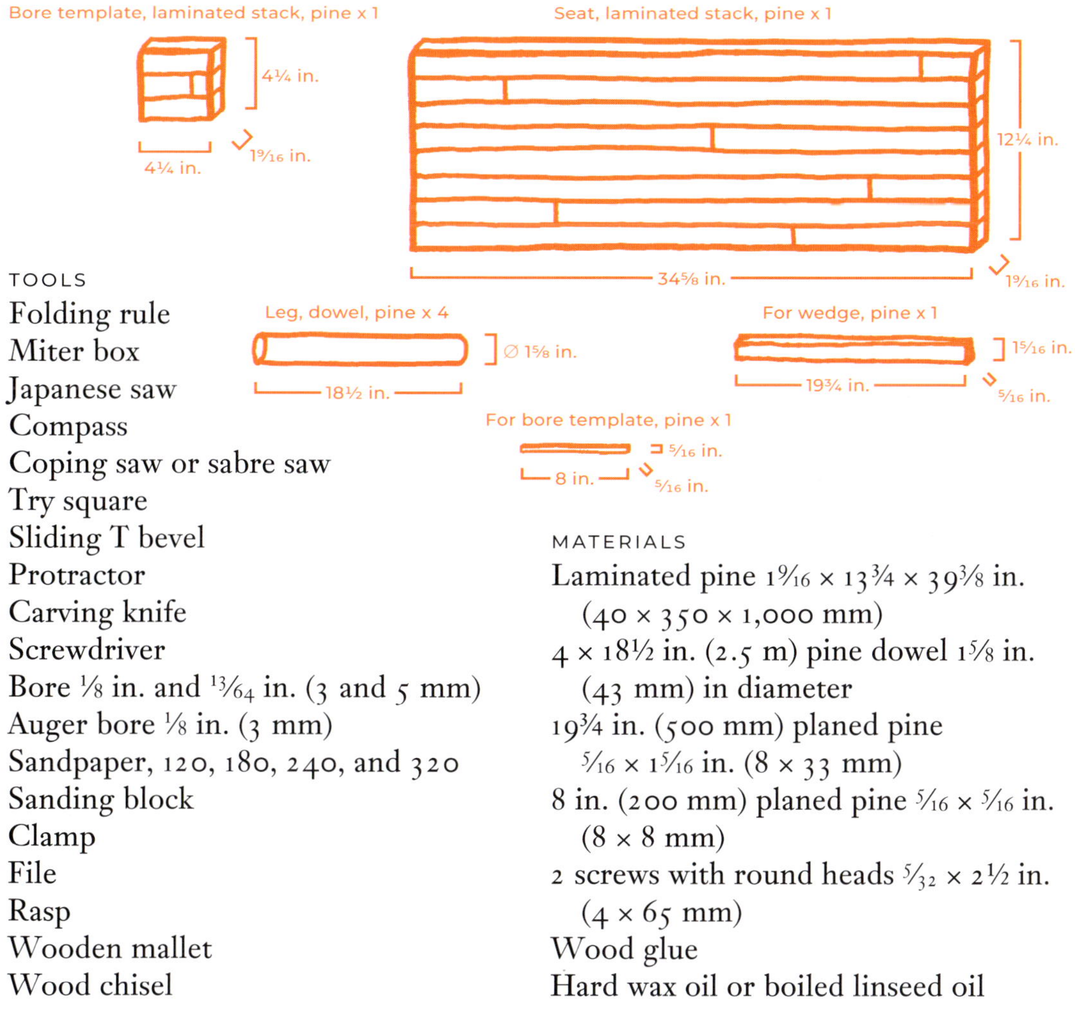

TOOLS

Folding rule
Miter box
Japanese saw
Compass
Coping saw or sabre saw
Try square
Sliding T bevel
Protractor
Carving knife
Screwdriver
Bore 1/8 in. and 13/64 in. (3 and 5 mm)
Auger bore 1/8 in. (3 mm)
Sandpaper, 120, 180, 240, and 320
Sanding block
Clamp
File
Rasp
Wooden mallet
Wood chisel

MATERIALS

Laminated pine 1 9/16 × 13 3/4 × 39 3/8 in. (40 × 350 × 1,000 mm)
4 × 18 1/2 in. (2.5 m) pine dowel 1 5/8 in. (43 mm) in diameter
19 3/4 in. (500 mm) planed pine 5/16 × 1 5/16 in. (8 × 33 mm)
8 in. (200 mm) planed pine 5/16 × 5/16 in. (8 × 8 mm)
2 screws with round heads 5/32 × 2 1/2 in. (4 × 65 mm)
Wood glue
Hard wax oil or boiled linseed oil

STEP 1 At the lumberyard, ask for the pine sheets to be cut to the correct measurements, and keep any remnants.

STEP 2 Mark and cut the legs to correct length (see measurements on previous page). Cut in the miter box with a Japanese saw.

STEP 3 Chose which side of the leg you want to be up or down. For the nicest result, decide whether you want the annual rings to point outward or inward (see drawing below). When you've decided how the legs will be placed, you can mark the top of each leg—RB (right back), LF (left front), etc.

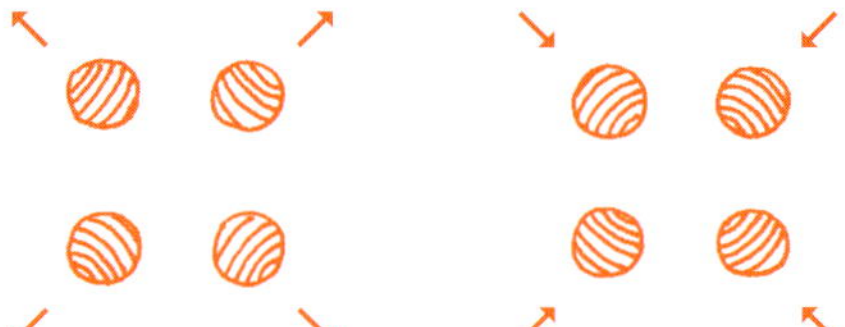

STEP 4 Now round the feet (see technique on page 40). When you've finished rounding, sand each foot and leg with 240-grit sandpaper.

STEP 5 Once the feet are finished, you can carve the back neck and tongue at the top of the leg. Begin by drawing a line around the dowel 2¾ inches (70 mm) down from the end. Then draw a circle on the end wood, 1³⁄₁₆ inches (30 mm) in diameter, with a compass. Make sure that the circle is centered. Next, carve away the material between the markings until you have a tongue that is evenly thick all the way down. Carve only a little material at a time, carving an even layer until you're down to the correct dimensions. Do the same on all four legs. To better control carving away enough material, you can bore a hole with a 1¼-inch (30mm) bore in a waste sheet and test to make sure the leg fits in.

STEP 6 Now draw a line straight across the top of the tongue, through the center marking. The line shows where you'll cut for the wedge. At this point, it's important that you double-check the order of the legs so that the cut lands in the right place. The cut should break the annual rings at an approximately 45° angle (see drawing below). Continue the line for 2⅜ inches (60 mm) down on each side of the tongue.

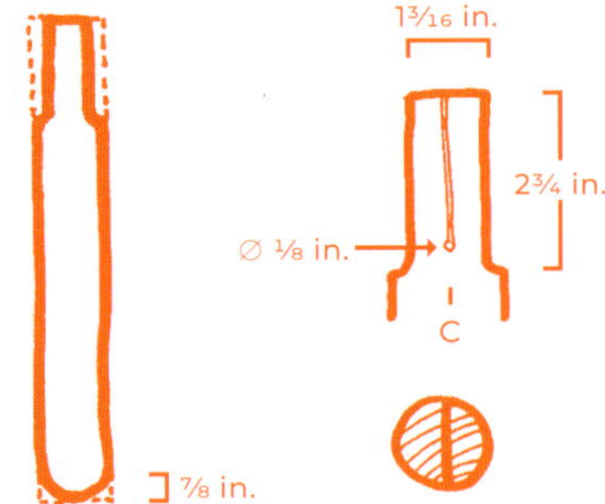

STEP 7 Bore a hole with the ⅛-inch (3mm) bore where the line ends. Work carefully so the hole will be straight and come out at the end of the line on the other side of the tongue. Next, use the Japanese saw to cut along your drawn marking. The cut should end at the bore hole, so cut carefully at the

end to make sure that you don't cut too deeply. The bore hole is made there to prevent the tongue from splitting when you hammer in the wedge later. Repeat on the rest of the legs.

STEP 8 Now the legs are ready for gluing, and it's time to begin making the seat. Keep the seat as a rectangle while you bore the holes for the legs. It's a good idea to maintain straight angles when you're measuring and making right-angle lines. Draw the markings on the underside of the seat. Draw half circles in the ends with a compass, the center for the hole for each leg, and 45° lines. Use a try square with a 45° angle setting (see measurements on drawing).

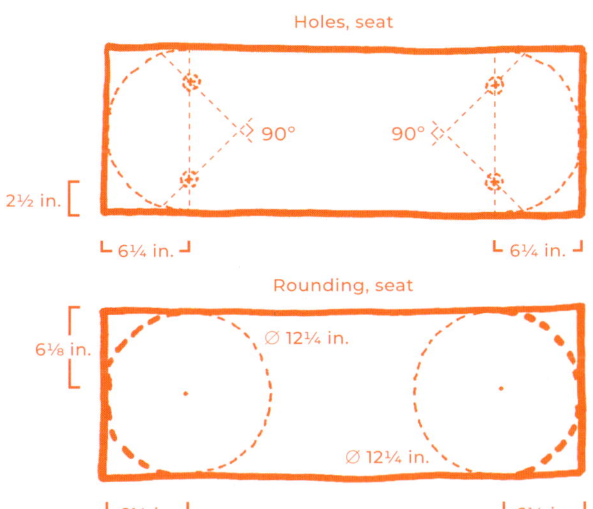

STEP 9 Now make a template for boring the legs. Mark and cut a square 4⁵⁄₁₆ × 4⁵⁄₁₆ inches (110 × 110 mm) from the pine sheet's waste wood. Cut freehand or against a sawing block and cut as perpendicularly as you can. Make a line straight across over the block, stretching from corner to corner. Mark where the holes should be bored (see measurements on drawing). Bore with a 1¼-inch (30mm) auger bore. It's important that you bore as vertically as possible. You can use a try square to make it easier to see that you're holding the bore straight.

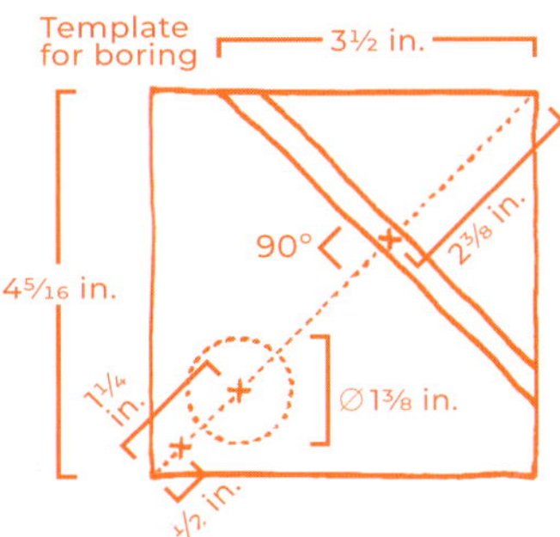

STEP 10 Glue the ⁵⁄₁₆-by-⁵⁄₁₆-inch (8 × 8mm) slat to the underside of the bore template. Draw the lines to follow, using the measurements in the illustration above, and then glue down the slat. It's important that it aligns with the markings so it won't be crooked. When the glue has dried, you can cut away anything sticking out from the slat with a Japanese saw.

STEP 11 Bore the other two holes with a ¹³⁄₆₄-inch (5mm) bore.

STEP 12 Now you can bore the holes for the legs, using the template for boring as a guide. Screw the template to the underside of the seat with ⁵⁄₃₂-by-2½-inch (4 × 65mm) screws so that the diagonal lines on the template align with the diagonal lines on the seat, and your markings on the seat indicating where you'll bore are at the center of the hole on the template.

Secure the seat on your work surface with a clamp and place a sheet of wood under it that you can bore down through when the bore comes through the seat. It's important to securely clamp the seat so the wood won't spray out as the bore goes through. Then, bore at full speed on the screwdriver. The screwdriver will probably tear the template before you go all the way through the seat, so remove the template and then bore directly into the hole, which, by then, should be deep enough to work at a straight angle. Be careful to maintain the angle as on the template, through the entire hole. If you possibly can, look into the hole as you bore and make sure you're holding it at the correct angle all the way through the hole. It can be difficult to see when you can only check from above. Bore all four holes the same way.

STEP 13 Check to make sure the legs fit into the holes and that the angles look good. In all likelihood, not all four holes will, unfortunately, have the same angle. It's almost impossible to do this precisely when boring freehand, because the smallest mistake in the angling will affect how the leg sits. Luckily, there are tips for how you can adjust the legs into the correct position. Use a sliding T-bevel gauge and place it against one of the legs, centered on the diagonal line. Lock in the leg's angle and then check the angle against those on the other legs. If one of the legs is at an angle that is either too small or too big, you can bore into the hole freehand and angle the bore in the correct direction that the leg should be at. Test by inserting the leg again and making sure that there is a difference. Most often, only a very small adjustment needs to be made for all to be right. The hole now is slightly oval, and the leg won't automatically go in at the angle you want it at, but as long as the leg is held at the angle you want, you should be satisfied. You can also adjust to the correct angle when you glue later.

You can also make adjustments by carving away a little material on the legs. Make sure you carve on the correct side.

Use the folding rule to make sure that all the legs stick out by the same amount on the topside of the seat. If any of the legs stick out less than the others, you can carve away a little bit more from the "neck" of the leg. Clearly mark which leg will sit in which hole.

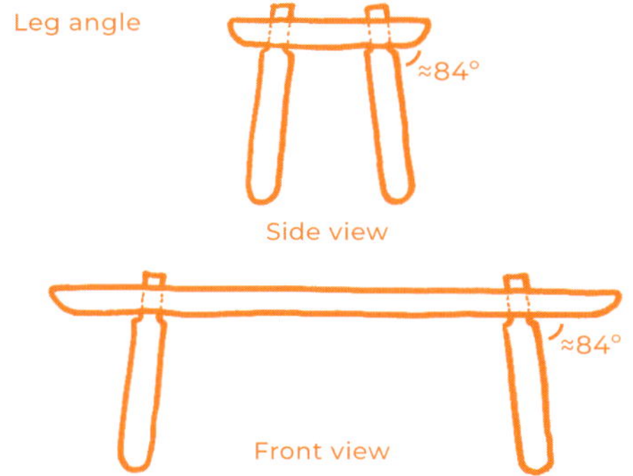

STEP 14 Once all the legs are fitted, you can begin shaping the seat. Begin by using the coping saw to cut the rounding on the ends.

Then, make a line running all around the underside of the seat, 1½ inches (40 mm) in from the edges. This indicates how far in you'll make the rounding. Next, make a template on paper or cardboard of a quarter circle with a 1$\frac{9}{16}$-inch (40mm) radius, the same way as you did when you rounded the legs.

STEP 15 Securely clamp the seat on the work surface, with the underside up, and begin shaving off the edge. Begin with a rasp or plane if you have one. Throughout, check against the template to make sure you haven't taken too much off. When you're close to the finished rounding, change to a file instead of the rasp or plane. Finish with 120-grit sandpaper without a block, or with a rather soft block, and then sand with 180-grit sandpaper.

STEP 16 Now you can make the wedges for the legs: Use the planed pine—$\frac{5}{16}$ × 1$\frac{5}{16}$ inches (8 × 33 mm)—and form a wedge with a carving knife or rasp and file on one end. You can narrow about 2 inches (50 mm) from the end (see illustration). When you're finished with the wedge shape, you can cut the wedge from the planed pine. Cut it in a miter box with a Japanese saw. Then, make a matching wedge from the same end and the other two from the other end. This way, the annual rings will point in two different directions on the ends of the wedges, which is desirable because the legs have annual rings pointing in two different directions, and you'll want to have a zigzag pattern on the pegs when you hammer them into the wedge (see illustration below).

Next, carve for the width of the wedges so they have the same measurements as the tongue on the leg they will sit in.

STEP 17 Now you can glue the legs into the seat. In this case, you can't do dry gluing beforehand, so prepare as much as you can ahead of time. Have the glue, wooden mallet, and sliding T bevel ready. Lay the seat with the underside upwards and a spacer under-

neath, so the tongues won't damage the work surface when you insert the legs. Carve various sizes of shavings and lay them in a pile. Place a leg next to the hole it'll sit in, and keep track of which wedge goes in which leg.

Begin by putting glue into the hole in the seat. You can be generous with the glue. Also put glue on the tongue of the leg before you insert it into the hole. Insert all the legs and then turn the stool and twist the legs so the path of each tongue is angled correctly.

Then, turn the stool back over again, with the legs upward, and double-check the angles with the sliding T-bevel gauge. On the legs for which you adjusted the holes on the wedge, you can wedge in shavings with glue on them on the side of the leg where it gaps. Wedge in as many shavings as possible. Once you have done that, you can turn the stool over, put glue on the wedges, and drive them into the legs with a wooden mallet. Hammer them in as far as you can. You should place

a block between the mallet and wedge when you hit it, to prevent the wedge from splitting. You must do all these steps in about 10-15 minutes. Then let the glue dry for about 40 minutes.

STEP 18 Once the glue has dried, you can use a flush or Japanese saw to cut off any parts of the tongues that stick out. Then use a chisel or file to make the tongues even with the seat. Turn the stool over and cut away anything sticking out from the shavings with either a knife or chisel. Sand away all the lines and markings with 120-grit sandpaper and then sand the entire stool with 240-grit sandpaper. If the legs are a little uneven and the stool wiggles, you can just file off a little under the feet of the two legs that touch the ground until all four legs stand evenly.

STEP 19 Finish the surface with either hard wax oil or boiled linseed oil. Use a rag or sponge to apply a layer of oil; wipe off any excess and let dry. Sand down with 320-grit sandpaper and then apply another layer of oil.

SHOE RACK

This shoe rack was inspired by a bench that Formbruket designed for Granit. It has two racks for shoes and is topped with a bench so you can sit down when you're tying your shoelaces. You can make the bench shorter or longer to fit your home, but if you make it longer, you'll need to purchase wider dowels, with a diameter of perhaps 1 or 1¼ inches (25 or 30 mm).

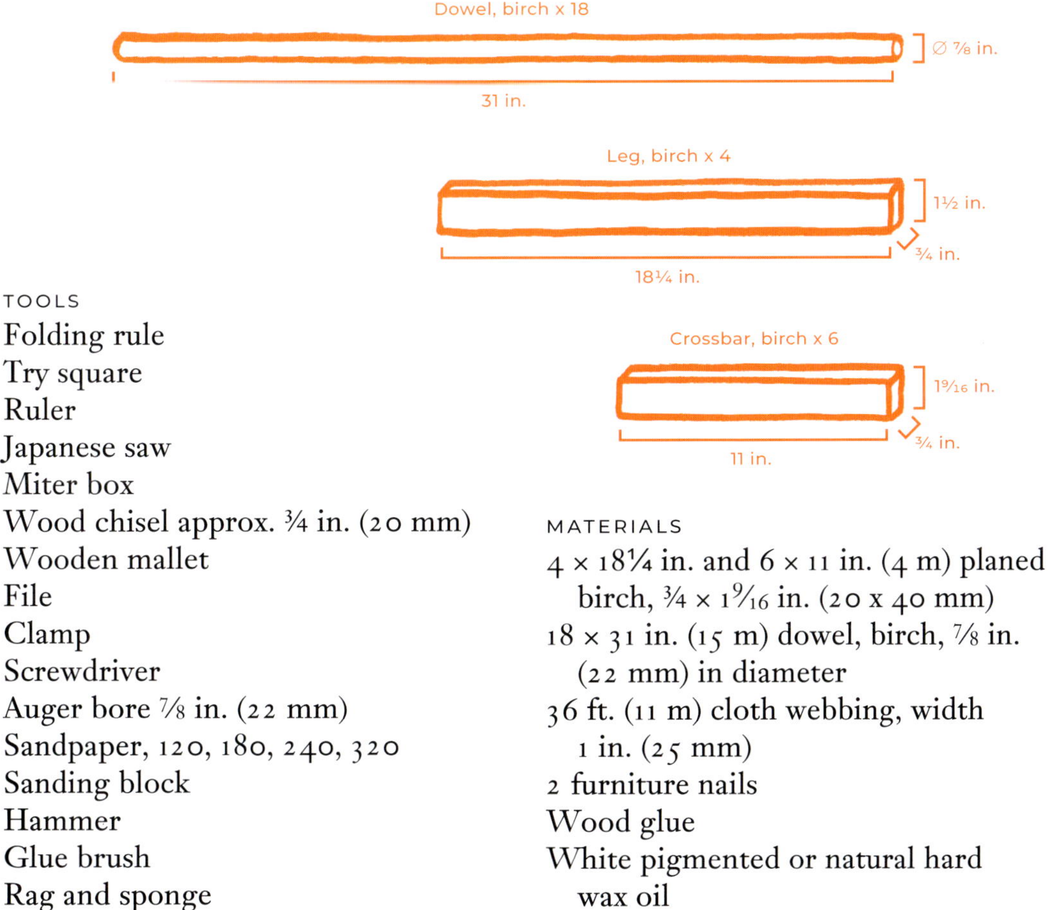

TOOLS

Folding rule
Try square
Ruler
Japanese saw
Miter box
Wood chisel approx. ¾ in. (20 mm)
Wooden mallet
File
Clamp
Screwdriver
Auger bore ⅞ in. (22 mm)
Sandpaper, 120, 180, 240, 320
Sanding block
Hammer
Glue brush
Rag and sponge

MATERIALS

4 × 18¼ in. and 6 × 11 in. (4 m) planed birch, ¾ x 1 9/16 in. (20 x 40 mm)
18 × 31 in. (15 m) dowel, birch, ⅞ in. (22 mm) in diameter
36 ft. (11 m) cloth webbing, width 1 in. (25 mm)
2 furniture nails
Wood glue
White pigmented or natural hard wax oil

STEP 1 Cut all the pieces to the correct lengths, both the planed birch and the dowels (see drawing for measurements on previous page). Cut with the Japanese saw and use the miter box for 90° cuts.

STEP 2 The two sides will be joined with a lap joint technique. Use the try square to mark where you'll make the cutouts, and follow the instructions for a lap joint on page 31 (see drawings below for measurements).

Lap joint, legs

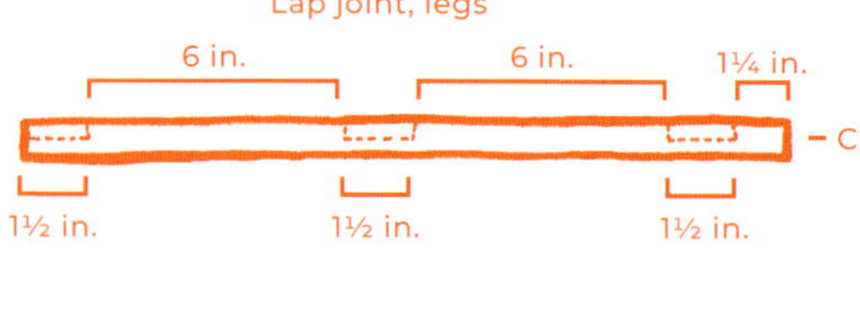

Lap joint, crossbars

8 in.
C
1½ in.
1½ in.

STEP 3 Arrange the pieces as they will be joined, and mark them so you can see what will be where. Make any adjustments to the fit with either a chisel or file until all the pieces fit together well.

STEP 4 Once you're satisfied with the fit of all the joints, you can glue the sides together. Begin with one side. If you have enough clamps, you can glue all five pieces at the same time—just make sure beforehand that you have everything prepared and know which piece fits to which. If you don't have enough clamps, you can glue one or a pair of pieces at a time. Apply the glue to the contact surfaces and clamp the join or joins together. Use the try square to ensure that the angles are at 90°. Leave the pieces clamped for about 30 minutes. Repeat the process with the other sidepieces.

STEP 5 Now both sides are joined. Choose which side you think is best and face it outward. As you can see, the sidepieces look a bit different since the crossbars overlap the legs on one side and the legs overlap the crossbars on the other side. I decided to have the side where the legs overlap the crossbars turned out. When you decide which are the inside and outside pieces, you can mark the inside where you want to bore holes for the dowels (see measurements on drawing).

STEP 6 Bore the holes with a ⅞-inch (22mm) auger bore, ⅝ inch (15 mm) deep. Bore as vertically as you can. Use a small try square to help with alignment if you think it makes it easier.

STEP 7 Sand off any particles on both ends of the dowels with 120-grit sandpaper so it'll be easier to get into the holes and the glue will have somewhere to go in.

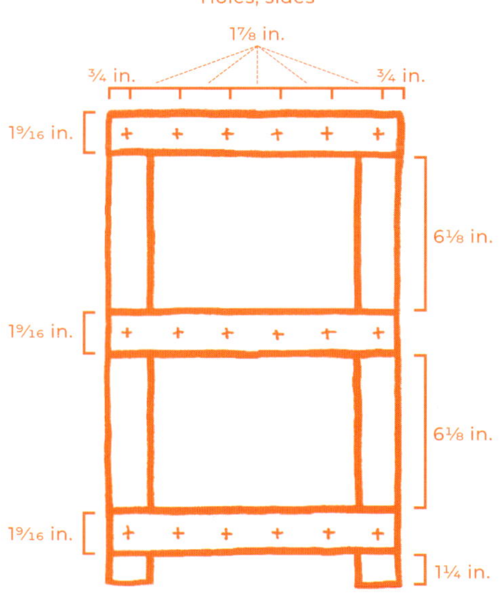

STEP 8 Sand all the joins on the sidepieces to remove any unevenness. Begin with 120-grit sandpaper for any big areas of unevenness. Then, continue with 180-grit sandpaper and sand all the sides. Break the edges by using a sanding block, sanding in the direction of the grain.

STEP 9 Now you can securely glue all the dowels into the sidepieces. Both sides must be glued firmly at the same time so you can ensure that the shoe rack won't be crooked. You have to do this as quickly as possible, so make

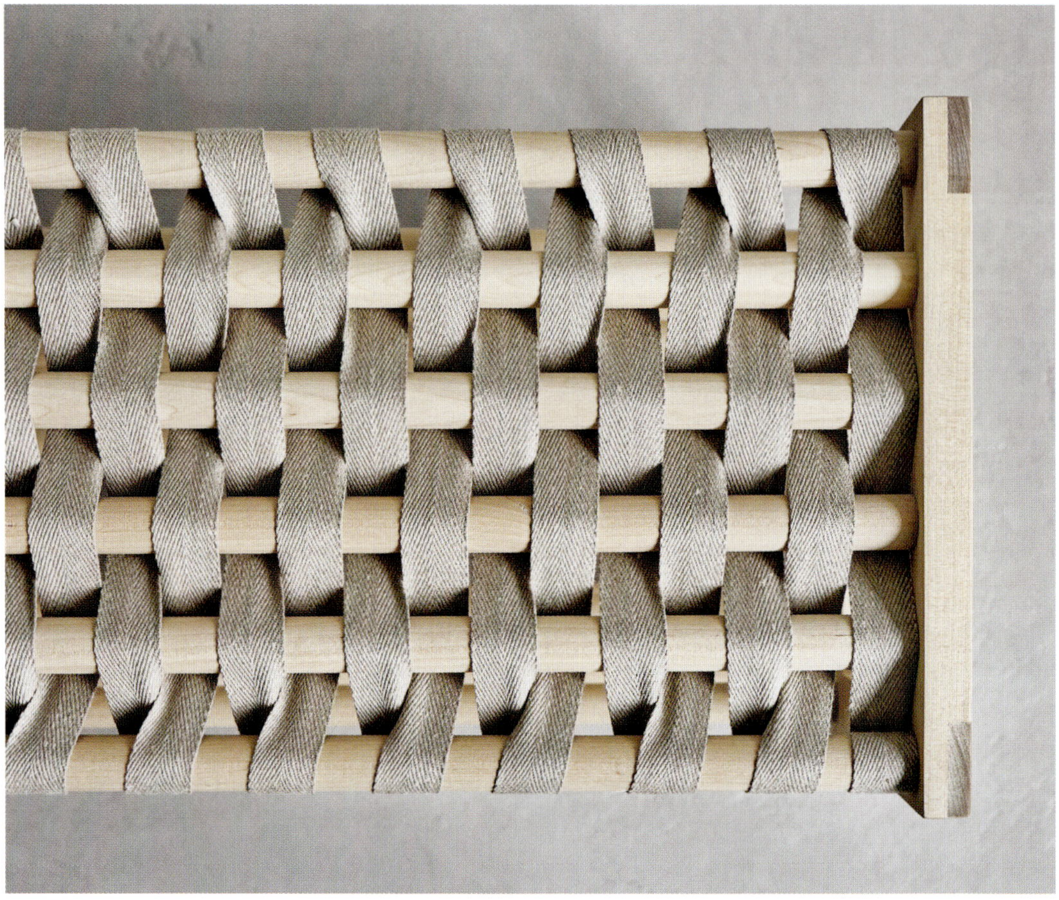

sure that you have everything you need for gluing before you begin: glue, brush, wooden mallet, and a block for driving in. The entire procedure must be done in about 15 minutes, so it helps to have two of you! Lay one sidepiece on the floor and apply glue into the holes. Swirl the brush in the holes to spread out the glue, working as fast as you can. Set the dowels in the holes and use the wooden mallet to drive them in until they are at the bottom of the holes. When everything has been set in correctly, you can work on the opposite side. This is the point at which it can be difficult to get each of the 18 dowels into its respective hole simultaneously. Leave the sidepiece on the floor, with the dowels pointing up. Apply glue into the holes on the other sidepiece, exactly as you did on the first side. Next, place it over the dowels and arrange the dowels into the holes, one after the other. Make sure that each dowel is set into the correct hole. The dowels you've already set in may try to jump out when you place a new dowel, but you just need to have patience. Once all the dowels are in their respective holes, you can tamp each one in on the top with the wooden mallet, holding a wood block between mallet and dowel to prevent any marks on your furniture. Once all the dowels are set into the bottom, you can stand the shoe rack up onto a completely flat underlay, with "the feet" downward. Make sure that all four feet touch the ground. If they don't, you'll need to twist the shoe rack to eliminate any crookedness. Twist in the direction opposite the crookedness. Then, set the rack on the ground and place a few stacks of books on top so all the feet are in contact with the ground. Wipe away any excess glue.

STEP 10 Once the glue has dried, sand the entire rack with 240-grit sandpaper. Then, oil it with white pigmented or natural hard wax oil. Use a rag or sponge and then wipe off any excess glue with a damp rag. When the oil is dry, you can sand it lightly with 320-grit sandpaper before applying the next layer of oil. Apply the oil as previously.

STEP 11 After the second application of oil has dried, it's time to weave in the webbing for the seat. Begin by nailing one end of the band to the topside of one of the outer dowels. Position the furniture nail about ⅝ inch (15 mm) in from the end. Twist the band once around the dowel so the nail is hidden, and then begin weaving. Tension the band tightly so it'll be nice and firm, but don't add too much tension or the dowels will begin to misalign. When you've woven the band all the way around, nail the other end down firmly underneath the dowel, using your finger as a marker. Trim the webbing to an inch (a couple of centimeters) or so from your finger. Fold in the end of the band so it's a little more than one wrap around the dowel, and then nail it in with a furniture nail on the underside. Adjust the webbing band so it's all aligned nice and even.

持ち出し禁止

ORGANIZER

It takes me about 100 years to get out when I need to leave the house. The keys are in one place, my bag is in another, and my cap is nowhere to be seen. If you share my experience, then this organizer is what you need.

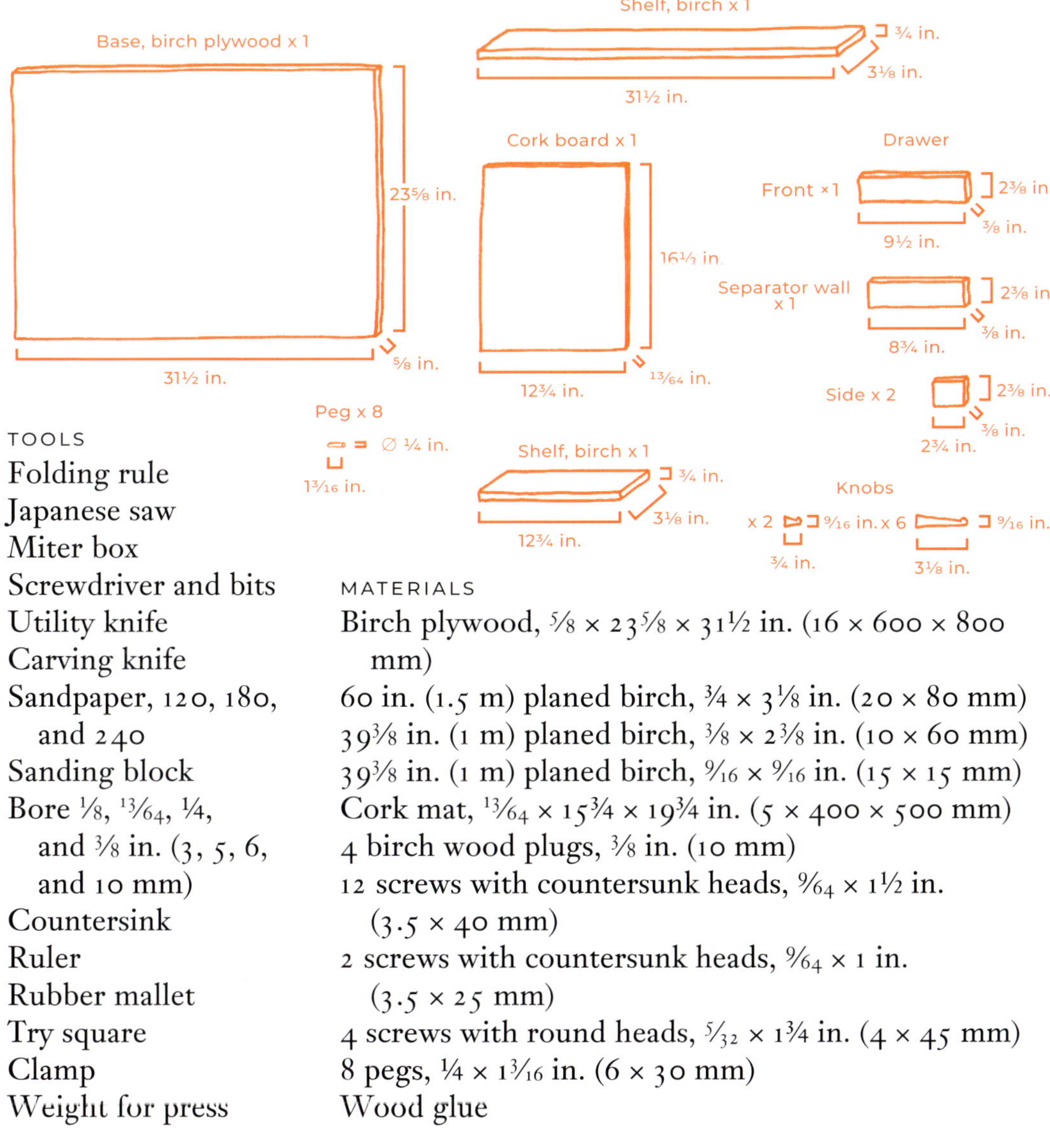

TOOLS

Folding rule
Japanese saw
Miter box
Screwdriver and bits
Utility knife
Carving knife
Sandpaper, 120, 180, and 240
Sanding block
Bore ⅛, 13⁄64, ¼, and ⅜ in. (3, 5, 6, and 10 mm)
Countersink
Ruler
Rubber mallet
Try square
Clamp
Weight for press

MATERIALS

Birch plywood, ⅝ × 23⅝ × 31½ in. (16 × 600 × 800 mm)
60 in. (1.5 m) planed birch, ¾ × 3⅛ in. (20 × 80 mm)
39⅜ in. (1 m) planed birch, ⅜ × 2⅜ in. (10 × 60 mm)
39⅜ in. (1 m) planed birch, 9⁄16 × 9⁄16 in. (15 × 15 mm)
Cork mat, 13⁄64 × 15¾ × 19¾ in. (5 × 400 × 500 mm)
4 birch wood plugs, ⅜ in. (10 mm)
12 screws with countersunk heads, 9⁄64 × 1½ in. (3.5 × 40 mm)
2 screws with countersunk heads, 9⁄64 × 1 in. (3.5 × 25 mm)
4 screws with round heads, 5⁄32 × 1¾ in. (4 × 45 mm)
8 pegs, ¼ × 1³⁄16 in. (6 × 30 mm)
Wood glue

STEP 1 Have the birch plywood cut to specified measurements at the lumberyard.

STEP 2 Pre-bore the holes into the sheets, following the measurements on the drawing on page 127. The four holes in the corners should be bored with a ⅜-inch (10mm) bore through half of the thickness of the board and then with a 13⁄64-inch (5mm) bore through the board. All the other holes should be bored with a ⅛-inch (3mm) bore all the way through the board, and then these holes will be countersunk from the back.

STEP 3 Sand the front of the plywood with 180-grit sandpaper and then 240 grit. Use a sanding block and sand in the direction of the tree's grain.

STEP 4 Cut the cork mat to the measurements on the drawing on the previous page, using a utility knife and cutting along the edge of a ruler. Sand the cork surface that will face outward with 240-grit sandpaper and a sanding block; break the edges a little.

STEP 5 Glue the cork to the plywood: use small lines to mark where the cork should be glued onto the plywood. See the spacing in the illustration on page 127. Brush glue on the back of the cork, lay it in place on the plywood, lay the press sheet on top, and then add weights. The weights can be a stack of books, exercise weights, or something similar. Leave under the press for at least 30 minutes.

STEP 6 Mark and then cut the shelf to the specified length (see measurements on drawing). Make the marks using a try square and then cut with a Japanese saw in the miter box. Sand the cut surfaces with 120-grit sandpaper and a sanding block, and then sand the entire shelf with 240-grit sandpaper. Wait until later to break the edges with a knife.

STEP 7 Glue and firmly screw the shelf onto the plywood. Screw with 9⁄64-by-1½-inch (3.5 × 40mm) screws into the bored holes, from the back of the plywood. You don't need to bore into the shelf—just make sure that the screws go in at the center of the shelf. Check the drawings for placement and measurements.

STEP 8 Measure and then cut the pieces for the compartment that will be placed on the lower shelf. Mark the placement, using a try square, and then cut with a Japanese saw in the miter box. It's important that the cuts be at 90°.

STEP 9 Sand the ends of the drawer pieces with 120-grit sandpaper and a sanding block until you have a break, straight surface. Be careful not to round the edges.

STEP 10 Use a ¼-inch (6mm) bore to

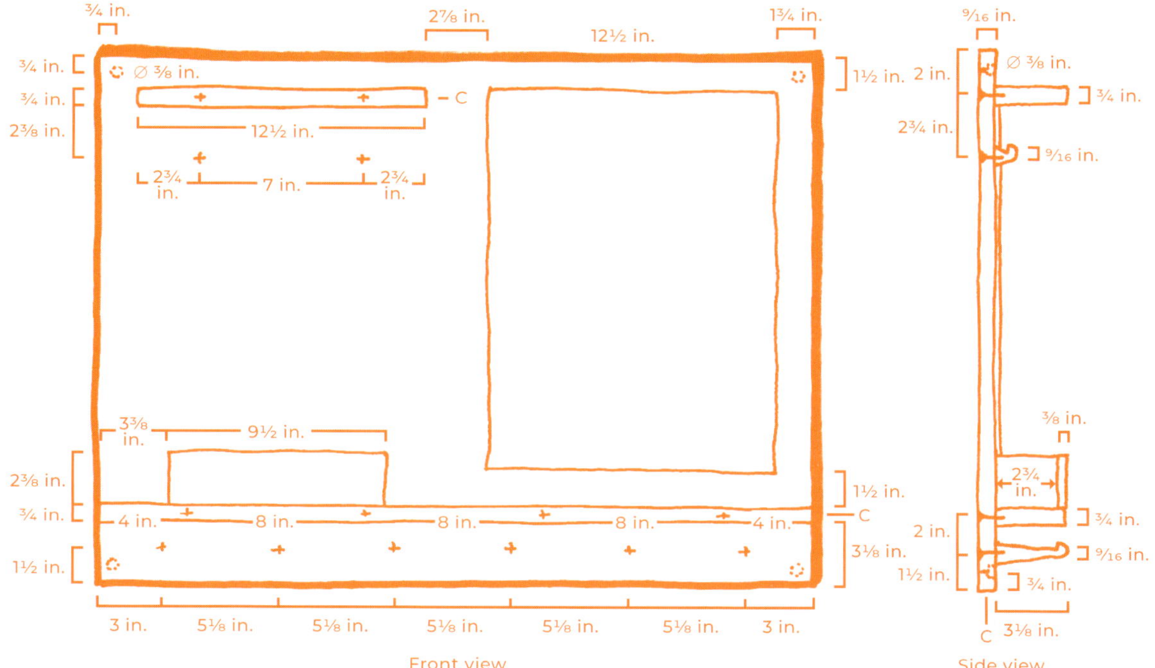

bore the holes for the pegs into the pieces, following the illustration. Glue the pegs into the holes that are in the end wood. Tap the pegs in with a rubber mallet and then wipe off any excess glue with a damp rag. Now assemble all the unglued parts to ensure that they fit together and that the pegs are in the right places. The tiniest little skewing will influence whether it'll all fit together well or not. If a peg didn't fit into a hole, you can carve a little away on the side of the peg until it fits. When all the pieces fit together, you can begin gluing. Start by gluing the separator panel to the sides. Apply the glue onto the contact surfaces and in the hole. Make sure that the pressure point from the clamp lands in a straight line centered on the separator panel. Wipe off any excess glue with a damp rag. Now glue the front together with the sides and wipe off excess glue.

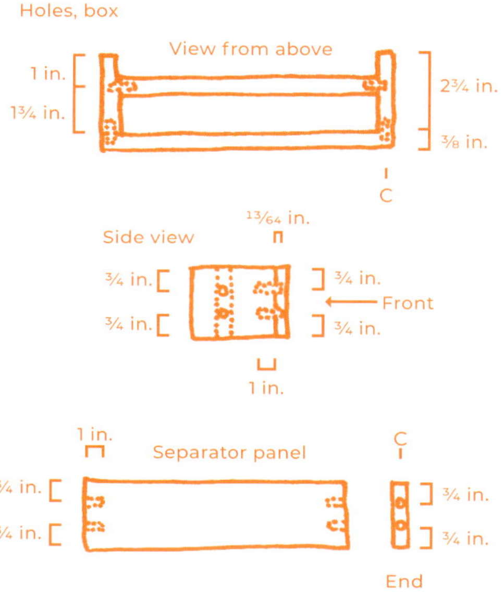

STEP 11 Sand the top, bottom, and sides with 120-grit sandpaper so they are even. Use a sanding block. Wait to sand the front. Bevel the edges on the inside of the compartment with a carving knife.

STEP 12 Glue the drawer to the shelf: Mark the placement of the drawer with short lines (see placement on drawing on previous page). Apply glue to the contact surfaces on the drawer and then set it in place. Clamp securely to the shelf with a clamp on each side and on the front. Wipe off excess glue as well as possible. Let sit in the press for about 30 minutes.

STEP 13 Once the glue is dry, sand the front of the drawer and the shelf so they are totally aligned with each other. Use a sanding block and 120-, 180-, and 240-grit sandpaper.

Bevel the edges and corners on the shelf and the drawer with a carving knife.

STEP 14 Now you can carve the knobs and shape them as you like. Keeping the birch pegs at their full length, mark out the length on a knob on one end and then make a perpendicular line all around the peg. Carve the knob as you want it to look, but do not carve over the markings. Next, cut the knob off at the markings while in a miter box. That way, you'll have a perpendicular cut on the knob. Now use the first knob as a template for the rest of the knobs (if you want them all to look alike) and work the same way. Mark, carve, cut. The same procedure applies to the two small knobs.

STEP 15 Once all the knobs have been carved, you can measure out for the center of the base. Make two diagonal lines from the end corners to form a cross. The center is where the two lines meet. Bore a hole at the center with a ⅛-inch (3mm) bore, about 9⁄16–¾ inch (15–20 mm) deep in the long knobs and ⅜ inch (10 mm) deep in the short ones.

STEP 16 Apply a drop of glue on the end of a knob and then screw it in firmly through the bored hole from the back of the plywood. Use a 9⁄64-by-1½-inch (3.5 × 40mm) screw for the long knobs and 9⁄64-by-1-inch (3.5 × 25mm) screws for the short ones.

STEP 17 Sand the sides and break the edges of the plywood sheet, using 240-grit sandpaper and a sanding block.

I decided not to finish the surface, but if you want to do so, feel free.

STEP 18 Screw the board to the wall through the four holes and then tap in the wood plugs with a rubber mallet.

TRAY TABLE

This is a simple collapsible table that you can use as a sideboard or sofa table. The design makes it suitable for trays you've bought if you like. The materials are calculated for one tray. If you want two, you'll need to double the amounts for the chipboard and cork mat.

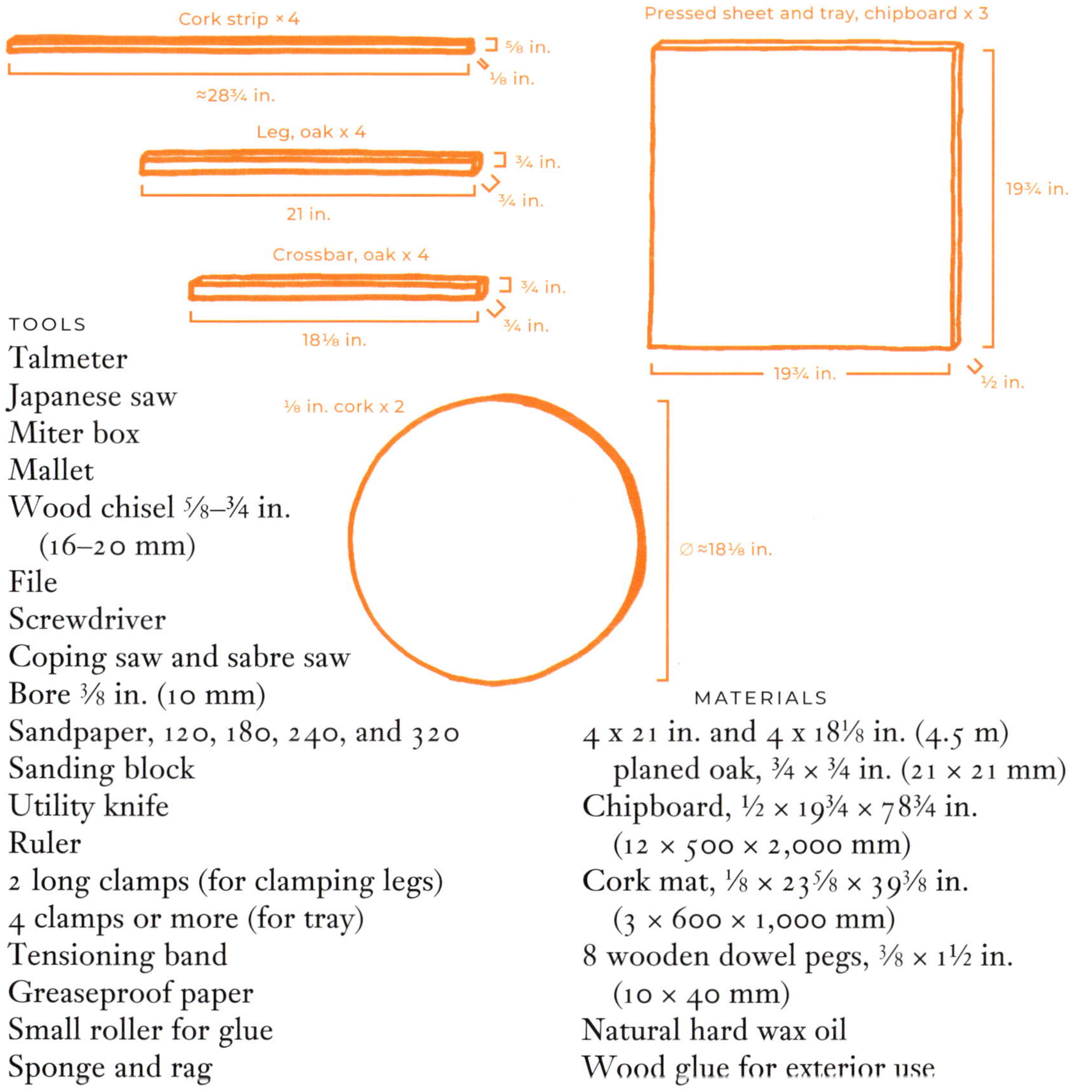

TOOLS

Talmeter
Japanese saw
Miter box
Mallet
Wood chisel ⅝–¾ in. (16–20 mm)
File
Screwdriver
Coping saw and sabre saw
Bore ⅜ in. (10 mm)
Sandpaper, 120, 180, 240, and 320
Sanding block
Utility knife
Ruler
2 long clamps (for clamping legs)
4 clamps or more (for tray)
Tensioning band
Greaseproof paper
Small roller for glue
Sponge and rag

MATERIALS

4 x 21 in. and 4 x 18⅛ in. (4.5 m) planed oak, ¾ × ¾ in. (21 × 21 mm)
Chipboard, ½ × 19¾ × 78¾ in. (12 × 500 × 2,000 mm)
Cork mat, ⅛ × 23⅝ × 39⅜ in. (3 × 600 × 1,000 mm)
8 wooden dowel pegs, ⅜ × 1½ in. (10 × 40 mm)
Natural hard wax oil
Wood glue for exterior use

STEP 1 Have the chipboard for the tray and the press pieces cut to the correct measurements at the lumberyard.

STEP 2 Mark and then cut the oak for the leg pieces to the correct lengths (see measurements on drawing on previous page). Use a try square when drawing and the miter box when cutting. The cuts should be at a 90° angle.

STEP 3 Mark where on each leg piece where you'll bore holes for the dowel pegs (see illustration). Then, bore the holes with a ⅜-inch (10mm) bore, 9/16 inch (15 mm) deep in the legs and 1 3/16 inches (30 mm) in the crossbars. Bore as vertically as possible. Secure the wood pieces with a clamp if you think it'll make it easier.

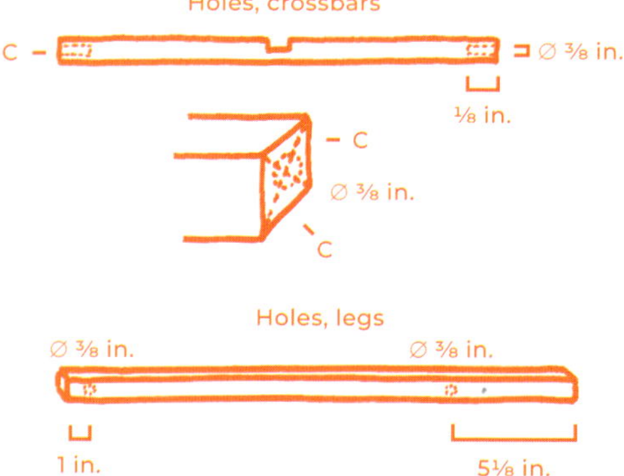

STEP 4 Make a lap joint on the crossbars (see drawing for measurements). You'll find the technique for a crossed lap joint explained on page 33. Make sure that the pieces fit into each other and lie nice and even. Use a file or wood chisel for fine adjustments if necessary.

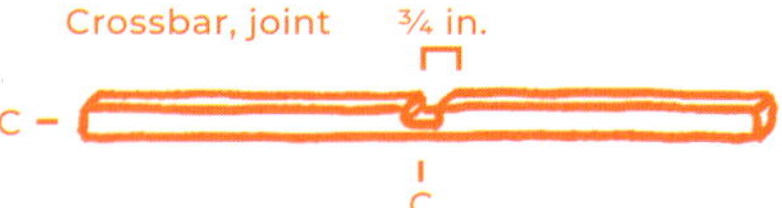

STEP 5 Now it's time to glue the leg pieces together. Begin by making a "dry" gluing and then actually glue the pieces. Start with one pair of legs. Apply glue into the holes and swirl it around with a small brush or stick. Tap the dowel pegs into the legs with a rubber mallet and then join the legs to the crossbars. Make sure that the cutouts end up in the same direction, and that both are turned either up or down. Clamp the pieces, making sure that the pressure is centered on the crossbar. Wipe off any excess glue with a damp rag. Once the glue is dry, you can remove the clamp and then glue the other leg pair. Keep in mind that these will be glued into the first pair (see illustration on next page). Also keep in mind that the cutouts should be turned to the opposite direction than that of the first pair, so that the joints can go together. If the first pair was turned upward, then this one should be turned down. Otherwise, work as for the first leg pair.

STEP 6 Sand the surfaces and joints on the legs. If there are any very uneven areas, you can begin with 120-grit sandpaper and then change to 180 and 240 grit. If everything is already nice and even, you can sand with 240 grit. Use a sanding block. When you've evened out all the surfaces, you can break the edges on the whole leg structure with 240-grit sandpaper.

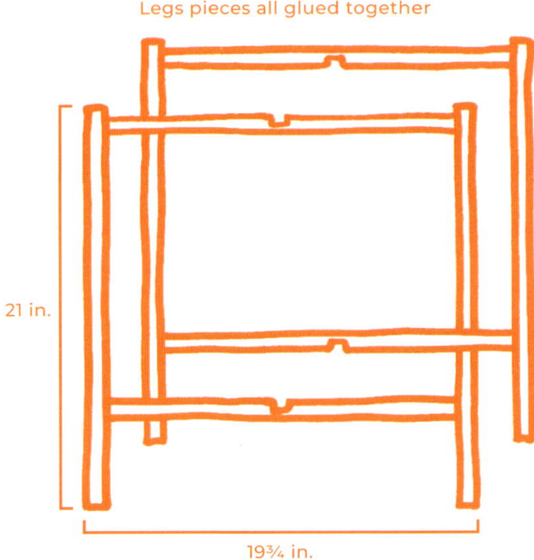

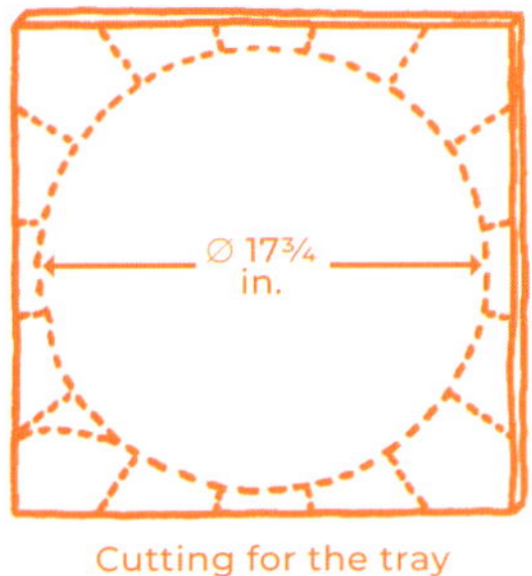

Cutting for the tray

STEP 7 Now you can make the trays. Begin by drawing a circle on the chipboard (see measurements on illustration). Use a compass or the compass function on a talmeter. If you don't have a talmeter or compass, it's good enough to set a screw in the center of the chipboard so it sticks up a bit, tightly tie a string around the screw, and then tie a pencil at the correct distance. Draw a circle by pushing the pencil around in a circle, always keeping the string taut. To make it easier to cut the circle, you can cut in "rays" from the edge into the circle. This way, the edge will be cut away bit by bit, instead of all in one piece (see illustration). Cut out the circle with either a coping saw or sabre saw.

STEP 8 Once you've cut out the circle, you can sand the edge with 120-grit sandpaper and a sanding block.

STEP 9 Cut two strips of cork mat with the utility knife, using a ruler as a guide (see measurements on illustration on page 131). These are the edge strips for the tray. Begin by applying glue to one strip; a little more than half the way around is enough. Place a strip of tape along all of one side of the cork strip and then apply wood glue to the other side of the cork strip. Make sure that the total strip length is covered with glue. Place the cork strip against the edge of the tray and, at the same time, pinch the tape firmly so it holds the strip in place. Make sure that the cork sticks out a little on both sides of the tray. Next, hold everything together with a tensioning band all around the edge. Let it sit in the press until the glue is dry. Remove the band and the tape strip and use the other cork strip to measure how long it should be by laying it against the edge that is not yet covered. Trim to correct length and then glue it on firmly as for the first strip.

STEP 10 Now the entire edge is covered with cork. Check the gluing to find out if there are any places not glued

securely. If so, just poke a little glue into any gaps and "clamp" it across with a strip of tape. When that glue has dried, you can sand down the cork edge so it aligns with the chipboard. Use 120-grit sandpaper and a sanding block. If there is too much cork to remove, you can cut it off with a utility knife and then sand. Do likewise all the way around on both sides of the chipboard.

STEP 11 Draw two circles on the cork that will be glued to the top and bottom of the tray: Lay the tray on the cork, a tiny bit (a few millimeters) in from the edge. Then, draw the tray's contours with a ballpoint pen. Angle the pen a little so the line is about 1/16 inch (2 mm) outside the round sheet. Make two identical circles. Cut out the circles on the cork.

STEP 12 Now you can glue the cork circles onto the tray. Prepare as much as possible in advance: Take out the glue and roller, press sheets, and greaseproof paper. Also lay out all the clamps. If you don't have many clamps, you'll need to prepare something else you can use as a weight on the sheets. This could be dumbbells, a large paint can, or something else heavy. Place one of the press plates on a work surface and cover it with a piece of greaseproof paper. Lay one of the cork circles on top. Apply glue to one side of the tray and use the roller to spread an even layer of glue. Don't be stingy with the glue. Lay the glue side down against the cork circle, making sure that the cork sticks out about the same way all around the entire tray. Glue the other side of the tray the same way and then lay the other cork circle on the tray. Cover with greaseproof paper and then add the second press plate. Clamp the whole assembly together, ensuring that the press comes over the trays, and not out on the edges outside the circle. Or place the weights on top. In any case, try to distribute the weight over the entire surface. You must do this in about 10–15 minutes—each step must happen quite quickly. Leave the assembly in the press or at least 40 minutes, preferably longer.

STEP 13 Sand off any cork sticking out from the edges, exactly as you did with the cork strips. Sand until the edge is fine and even. Poke a little glue into any gaps and secure with a strip of tape. Then, sand the entire tray with 120-, 180-, and 240-grit sandpaper. Round the edges a bit, using a sanding block.

STEP 14 Oil the leg frame and cork tray with natural hard wax oil. Let dry, sand with 320-grit sandpaper, and then sand and oil once more.

Liljevalchs

FOLDING SCREEN

If you don't live in a big place and want to divide a room, a good solution is a folding screen. This cane screen offers privacy without feeling heavy and closed in.

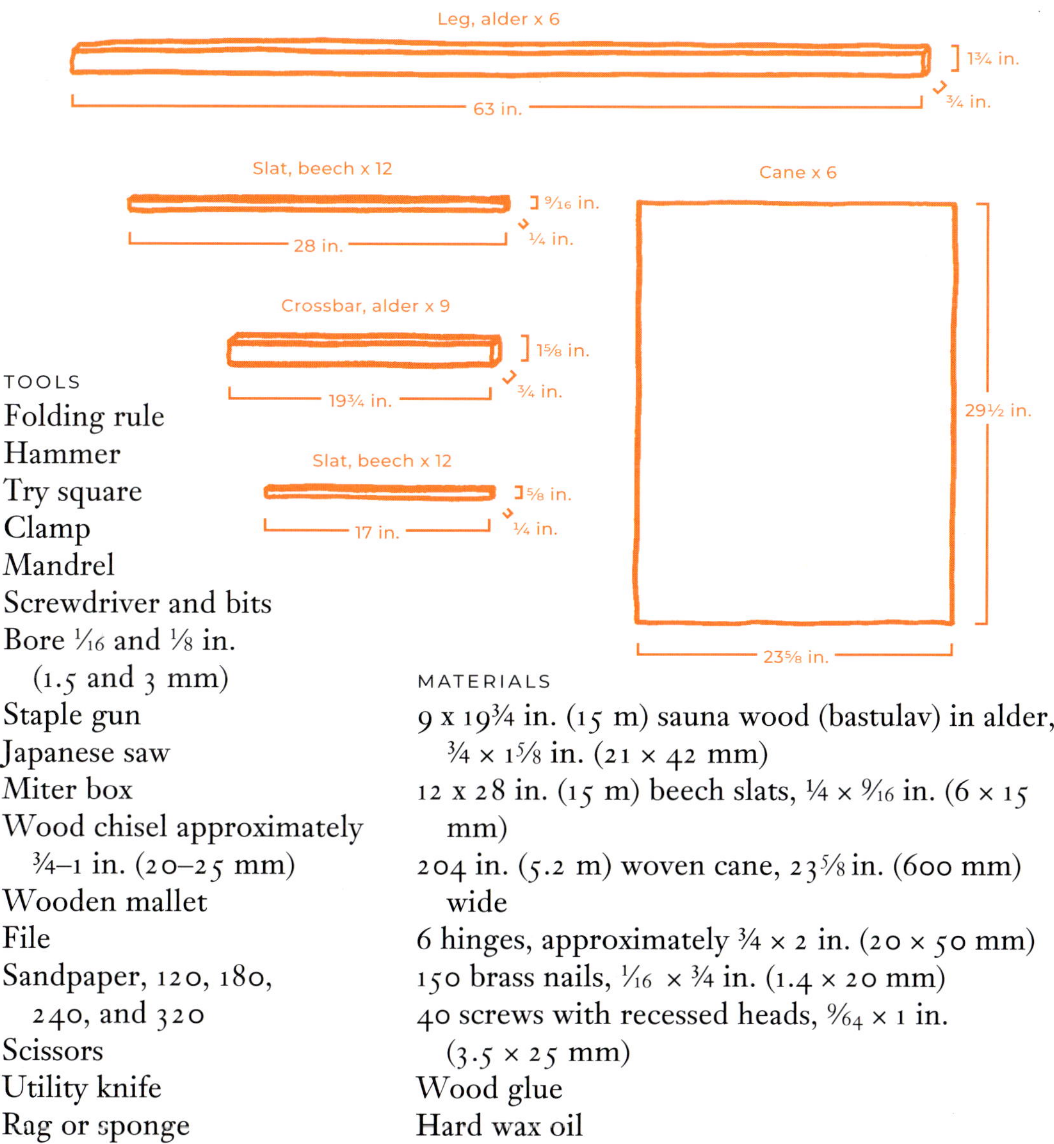

TOOLS

Folding rule
Hammer
Try square
Clamp
Mandrel
Screwdriver and bits
Bore 1/16 and ⅛ in. (1.5 and 3 mm)
Staple gun
Japanese saw
Miter box
Wood chisel approximately ¾–1 in. (20–25 mm)
Wooden mallet
File
Sandpaper, 120, 180, 240, and 320
Scissors
Utility knife
Rag or sponge

MATERIALS

9 x 19¾ in. (15 m) sauna wood (bastulav) in alder, ¾ × 1⅝ in. (21 × 42 mm)
12 x 28 in. (15 m) beech slats, ¼ × 9/16 in. (6 × 15 mm)
204 in. (5.2 m) woven cane, 23⅝ in. (600 mm) wide
6 hinges, approximately ¾ × 2 in. (20 × 50 mm)
150 brass nails, 1/16 × ¾ in. (1.4 × 20 mm)
40 screws with recessed heads, 9/64 × 1 in. (3.5 × 25 mm)
Wood glue
Hard wax oil

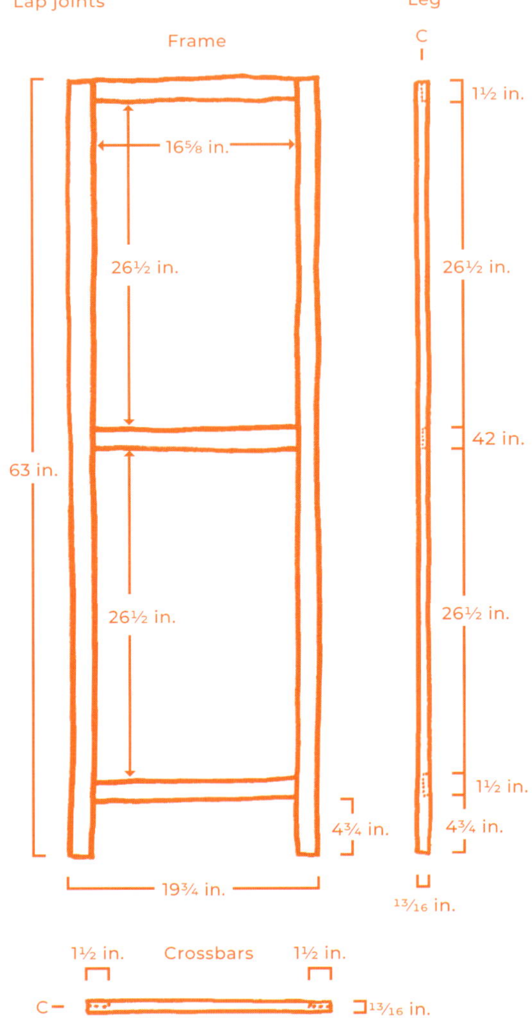

STEP 1 Measure and cut the materials to the specified lengths (see measurements on drawings on previous page). Use a try square when marking and a miter box for cutting.

STEP 2 Begin with the frame of alder slats. Mark the placement on the legs and crossbars for the joints (see illustration at right). Cut and cut out, following the description of the lap joint on page 31. Sort the legs and crossbars for the three frames into three piles and decide which piece will sit where. Mark the pieces so you'll know what goes where. This is necessary so you'll know how to adjust the fit.

STEP 3 Carefully adjust the joins so all the pieces will fit. Use a file or chisel.

STEP 4 Now you can glue the frames together. The number of joints you can glue at a time depends on how many clamps you have. If you only have one, glue only one joint at a time, if you have two, you can glue two, etc. Begin with one leg and glue on the crossbars one after the other. Apply the glue to the contact surfaces and clamp the pieces together. Alder is a rather soft type of wood, so place a small piece of wood or leather between the clamp and wood to prevent any pressure marks. Use the try square to make sure the pieces are at a 90° angle. Wipe off any excess glue with a damp rag. Continue the same way until the entire frame has been glued together, and then follow the same procedure for the other two frames.

STEP 5 Once all the frames have been glued, you can sand. Begin by sanding down any unevenness on the joints, with 120-grit sandpaper if there is much to sand down; otherwise, use 180 grit. Then, sand the entire frame with 240-grit sandpaper. Round the edges on the corners so they follow the rounding on the alder slats.

STEP 6 Finish the frames with natural hard wax oil. Apply it with a rag or sponge and wipe off any excess with a rag. Let dry and then sand with 320-grit sandpaper before you apply another layer of oil.

STEP 7 Pre-bore the holes in the beech slats with the 1⁄16-inch (1.5mm) bore, following the measurements on the drawing below. Be careful because the fine bore bit can break easily. It's good to have an extra in reserve.

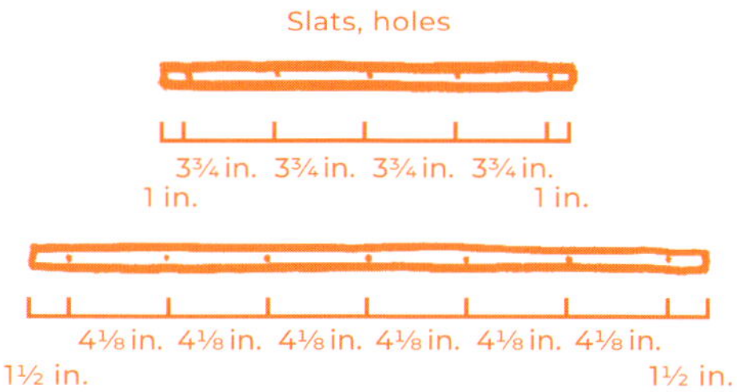

STEP 8 Round off the two edges that will face out, using 120-grit sandpaper, and then sand the slats with 240 grit. Break the edges at the ends and then oil all the slats with hard wax oil. One application of oil is sufficient here.

STEP 9 Cut the length of the cane, following the illustration on page 137. If your cane is wider than 23⅝ inches (600 mm), you can keep that width.

STEP 10 Begin with the top bars of all three frames, finishing them completely with slats, and then continue with the lower bars. Work as follows: Dampen the cane, either in a sink or bathtub. Let it sit and absorb the water for 5–10 minutes. Dry the cane with a hand towel so it's not soaking wet when you'll staple it into the frame.

STEP 11 The cane will have an obvious front side and backside. Hold it with the front turned toward you when you staple it on. Also decide which side you want to have as the front and back of the screen. Lay the cane with the same amount hanging over at the top, at the bottom, and on the sides. Begin stapling firmly in one top corner and then continue along the edges. The cane should be tensioned but not absolutely tight. It'll draw in and become tighter as it dries. Be careful to staple the cane aligned with the frame. Thanks to the block pattern in the cane, it's easy to staple the cane on straight, in line with the frame. The staples will later be covered with a 9⁄16-inch (15mm) slat, so make sure you only staple on the surface the slat will later cover. Space the staples closely, with a maximum of ⅜ inch (10 mm) between each. Proceed the same way around all three frames.

STEP 12 Nail the beech slats over the staples (see spacing from the outer edge of the frame on the drawing). You can first place the slats that will be nailed, to be sure that the slats will cover all the staples. Use pliers to remove any staples that aren't covered, and replace them with staples in the right place.

Nail through the pre-bored holes and use the mandrel for the last hit so that the nails will be aligned with the wood without leaving hammer marks on the slat.

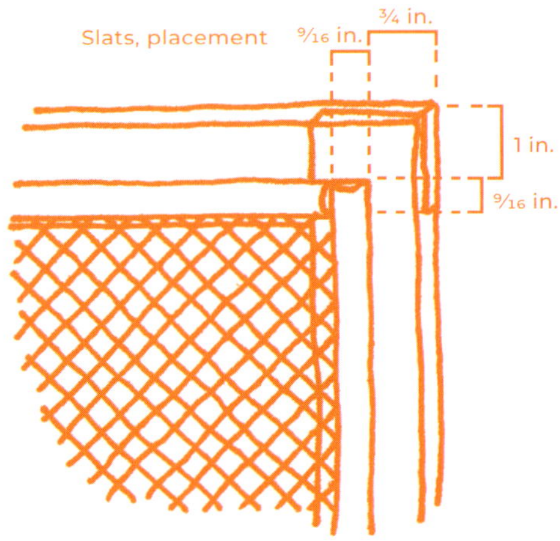

STEP 13 Make sure that you have a new, sharp blade on your utility knife, and cut off the cane along the outside of the slat by resting the blade against the edge of the slat. Do the same on the three top bars.

Work the same way with the cane and slats on the three lower bars.

STEP 14 Now the three screens are finished, and all that's left is to hinge them together. Because you want the screen to fold like an accordion, the joint on each hinge must be turned in one direction on one side and in the opposite direction on the other side. Begin from the frame in the middle and mark where the hinge will be placed. Look at the photos for the placement. Set the hinge against the frame and mark the holes. Pre-bore into the marks with a ⅛-inch (3mm) bore and then screw the hinge on.

STEP 15 Mark the hinge placement and pre-bore the holes on the other two frames. Screw them together with the middle frame.

BIRD FEEDER

It's so nice to observe the birds in the garden, so I made a bird feeder that will attract birds in both summer and winter. However, I wanted to break away from a traditional wooden bird feeder which often looks like a little house, so I asked an architect friend to sketch a somewhat different design. The birds are definitely worth a designer feeder!

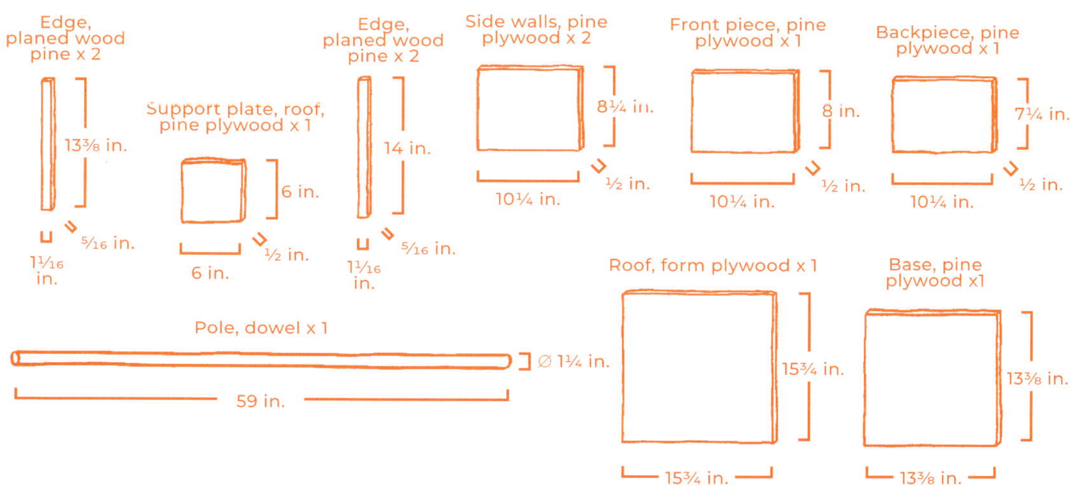

TOOLS

Japanese saw
Coping saw or sabre saw
Try square
File
Screwdriver and bits
Bore 5⁄64, 5⁄32, and ½ in. (2, 4, and 12 mm)
Countersink
Sandpaper, 120
Axe or knife
Brushes for paint and oil

MATERIALS

Pine plywood, ½ × 39⅜ × 47¼ in. (12 × 1,000 × 1,200 mm)
Form plywood, ½ × 15¾ × 15¾ in. (12 × 400 × 400 mm)
59 in. (1.5 m) dowel pole, 1¼ in. (33 mm) in diameter
78¾ in. (2 m) planed pine, 5⁄16 × 1¹⁄16 in. (8 × 27 mm)
25 wood screws, ⅛ × 1⅝ in. (3 × 42 mm)
4 screws, recessed head, ⅛ × ¾ in. (3 × 20 mm)
Wood glue for exterior use
Black paint
Boiled linseed oil

STEP 1 Cut the materials, following the illustrations. If you don't want to cut the wood sheets yourself, you can ask for it to be done at the lumberyard. You can still cut the angles for the two sidepieces and the cutouts by hand.

STEP 2 Draw the slits for the half-in-half cutouts on the under edge of the four wall pieces (see measurements on the drawings below). Use a try square.

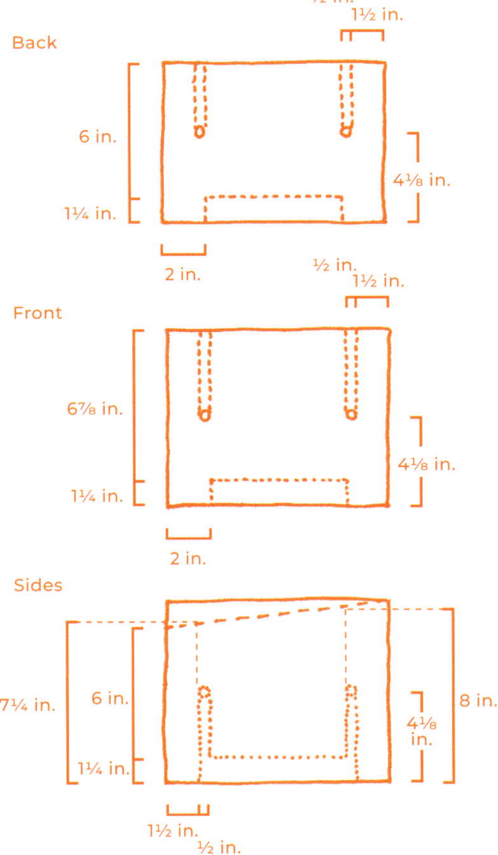

STEP 3 Bore holes with the ½-inch (12mm) bore down into the slits so that the cut ends with a rounding. Then, cut with a Japanese saw, following the markings. Use the sabre saw to cut away any jagged bits on the lower edge.

STEP 4 Once you've cut the slits and cutouts, you can check to make sure that the walls will fit together. If there is any tightness in places, use a file to make adjustments so the pieces fit.

STEP 5 When all four walls fit together, break the edges on the corners and sand the outside with 120-grit sandpaper. The walls do not need to be glued to each other, since they will be stable enough with just the half-in-half construction when the house is firmly screwed into the base.

STEP 6 When the walls are finished, you can proceed to the base. Pre-bore holes in the slats that will sit around the plate (see measurements on drawing on next page). Use a ⁵⁄₆₄-inch (2mm) bore. Also, pre-bore the holes in the bottom plate where the house and dowel will be attached (see measurements on drawing on next page). Countersink the holes for the house on the underside of the plate. Securely screw the slats onto the edges of the bottom plate with the wood screws.

STEP 7 Now the bottom plate and house walls are finished, and you can continue to the roof. Make sure that the support plate you'll screw onto the foot plate fits between the walls on the house. If it's too big, you can

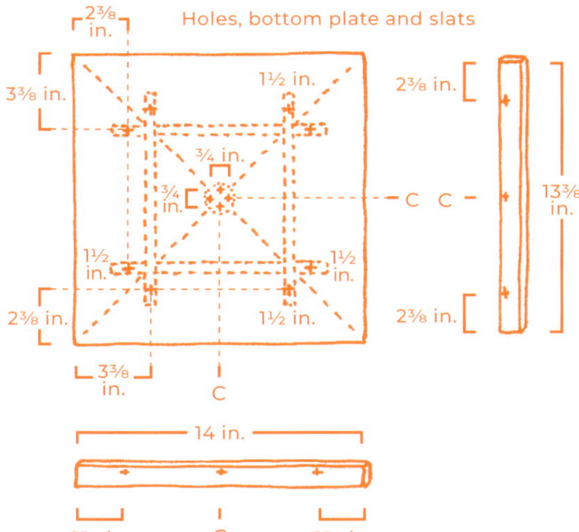

cut or file it a little so it fits. Pre-bore into the support plate with a 5/32-inch (4mm) bore, following the measurements in the illustration below, and countersink the holes. Next, firmly screw the support plate in the middle of the roof plate with the ⅛-by-¾-inch (3 × 20mm) screws. There should be an equal distance to the edge on all four sides.

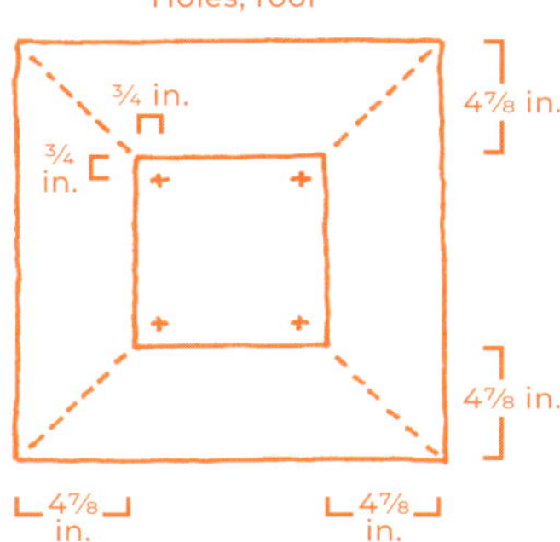

STEP 8 Sand the edges on the roof plate and smooth the edges. Paint the edges with the black paint so that the edges won't absorb moisture. You can oil the edges instead if you think it'll look nicer.

STEP 9 Now sharpen one end of the dowel pole to a point. It's most easily done with an axe, but you could also carve it with a knife. It doesn't matter how it looks, as it simply goes down into the ground.

STEP 10 Oil all the pieces except for the roof. The walls only need to be oiled on the outside. Use a brush to apply the oil, and let the oil dry for about 20 minutes. Then, wipe off any excess oil and apply another layer once the first layer has dried.

STEP 11 Drive the dowel pole into the ground where you want the bird feeder to be. Screw the bottom plate firmly onto the pole through the bored holes. Use wood screws. Next, securely screw the house onto the base: Center the house on the bottom plate and firmly screw it from the underside in the pre-bored holes. Use wood screws here also. Sprinkle on some seeds and put the lid on—now you only have to wait for the birds to arrive!

SWEET THURSDAY JOHN STEINBECK

BALCONY TABLE

If you have a balcony, it's lovely to have a table that folds down when not in use, so you have more space to move around in. Being able to fold the table down is also good when it rains, so the water runs off the wood. The table will then last much longer! I decided to use brass screws for my table because I think they look so nice against the oak.

TOOLS

Japanese saw
Miter box
Folding rule
Try square with 45° angle
Sandpaper, 120 and 240
Sanding block
Screwdriver and bits
Bore 3⁄32, 1⁄8, 9⁄64, 5⁄32, 13⁄64, and 3⁄8 in. (2.5, 3, 3.5, 4, 5, and 10 mm)
Countersink
Brush and rag

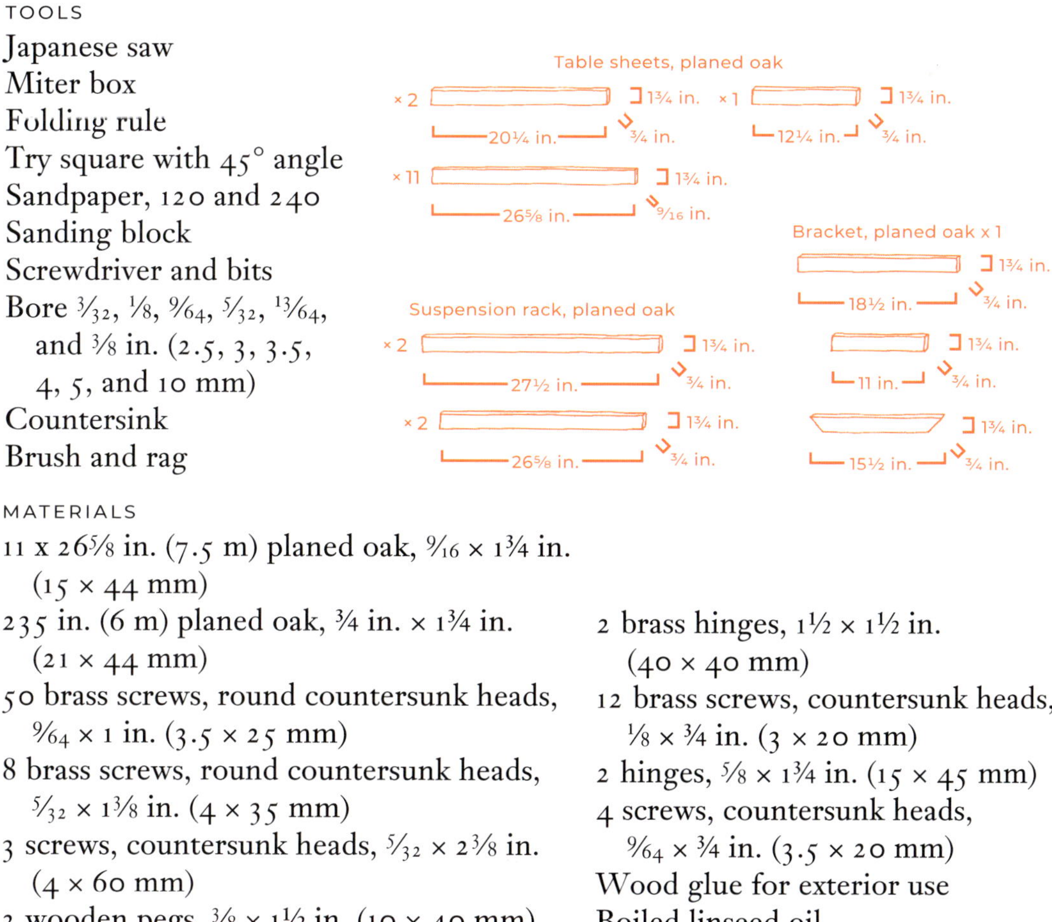

MATERIALS

11 x 26⅝ in. (7.5 m) planed oak, 9⁄16 × 1¾ in. (15 × 44 mm)
235 in. (6 m) planed oak, ¾ in. × 1¾ in. (21 × 44 mm)
50 brass screws, round countersunk heads, 9⁄64 × 1 in. (3.5 × 25 mm)
8 brass screws, round countersunk heads, 5⁄32 × 1⅜ in. (4 × 35 mm)
3 screws, countersunk heads, 5⁄32 × 2⅜ in. (4 × 60 mm)
2 wooden pegs, ⅜ × 1½ in. (10 × 40 mm)
2 brass hinges, 1½ × 1½ in. (40 × 40 mm)
12 brass screws, countersunk heads, ⅛ × ¾ in. (3 × 20 mm)
2 hinges, ⅝ × 1¾ in. (15 × 45 mm)
4 screws, countersunk heads, 9⁄64 × ¾ in. (3.5 × 20 mm)
Wood glue for exterior use
Boiled linseed oil

STEP 1 Measure and cut the materials to the correct lengths. Use a try square when you draw the markings, and cut in a miter box with a Japanese saw. The pieces for the bracket are at a 45° angle at both ends, so draw the lines for them with a try square with a 45° angle on the handle or with a sliding bevel. Then, cut in a miter box.

STEP 2 Once all the pieces have been cut, you can sort them into three piles: tabletop, bracket, and suspension rack.

STEP 3 Begin with the tabletop. Sand the ends of all the slats with 120-grit sandpaper and a sanding block. Then sand all the slats rather lightly with 240-grit sandpaper and break the edges and corners.

STEP 4 Pre-bore the holes in the slats for the tabletop with a 5⁄32-inch (4mm) bore and countersink the holes. Check the size of the screw heads and determine the depth of the countersinking to match that.

STEP 5 Lay the two supports, which will be parallel to each other under the tabletop on the work surface. Then lay the first tabletop slat edge to edge with the ends of the support. Measure so that the overhang of the slat is correct, following the illustration below, and then, with the 1⁄8-inch (3mm) bore, bore down into the support through the previously bored holes in the slat. Firmly screw the slat with 9⁄64-by-1-inch (3.5 × 25mm) screws, either brass or rustproof steel. If you choose brass screws, you must be very careful when you screw them in, because brass is a soft metal and oak is hard. A screw can break in the hole when you screw it in if you're not careful. If a screw does break, you can remove the screwhead and then bore again in the same place. Because brass is softer than the bore steel, the steel will bore away the piece still sitting in the hole. When you have screwed the first slat in firmly, you can lay out the next one. For an even gap between the slats, lay two spacers, 1⁄8

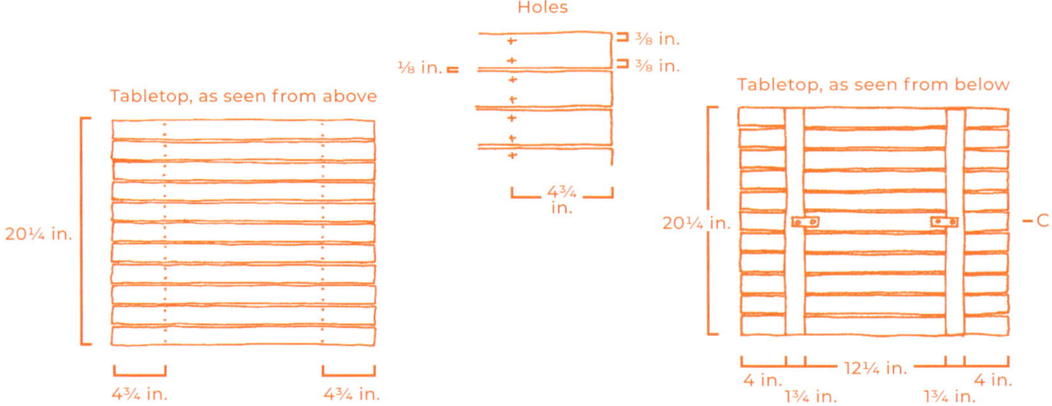

inch (3 mm) thick, between them, one at each end. Then, measure to ensure that the overhang is the same as on the first slat and the two slats are aligned. Use a try square to help. When the slats are in place, bore and screw exactly as you did for the first slat. Do likewise with the remaining slats.

STEP 6 Turn the tabletop and place it on the remaining support (see placement on drawing on previous plage). Lay a hinge on both ends so they overlap the joints, bore with a ⅛ in (3mm) bore, and firmly screw in a 9⁄64-by-¾ inch (3.5 × 20mm) screw.

STEP 7 Turn Now the tabletop is ready, and you can begin with the support.

Bore the hole for the pins on the vertical part of the ends with a ⅜-inch (10mm) bore (see the illustration below). Bore ¾ inch (20 mm) deep as vertically as you can, then pre-bore with a 13⁄64-inch (5mm) bore in the vertical and horizontal parts as illustrated. Countersink the holes quite a lot, so that the screwheads don't stick up above the wood.

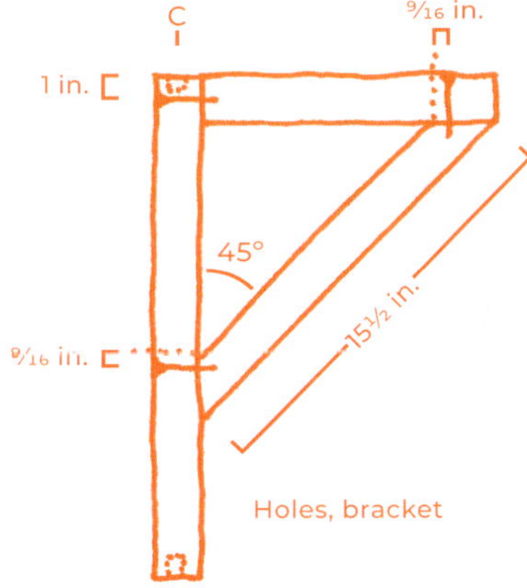

STEP 8 Arrange the three pieces as they will sit and bore through the bored holes with a ⅛-inch (3mm) bore. Glue and screw the three pieces to each other. Apply the glue to the contact surfaces and screw together with the 5⁄32-by-2⅜-inch (4 × 60mm) screws. Let dry.

STEP 9 Once the glue is dry, you can sand the glued joints and ends so they are even with 120-grit sandpaper and a sanding block. Then, sand the entire bracket with 240-grit sandpaper; break the edges.

STEP 10 Now begin assembling the support rack: Bore holes for the wooden pegs in the two horizontal pieces with a ⅜-inch (10mm) bore, 1 inch (25 mm) deep (see measurements on illustration below). Pre-bore the holes for the screws with a 13⁄64-inch (5mm) bore, following the measurements on the drawing. Countersink the holes.

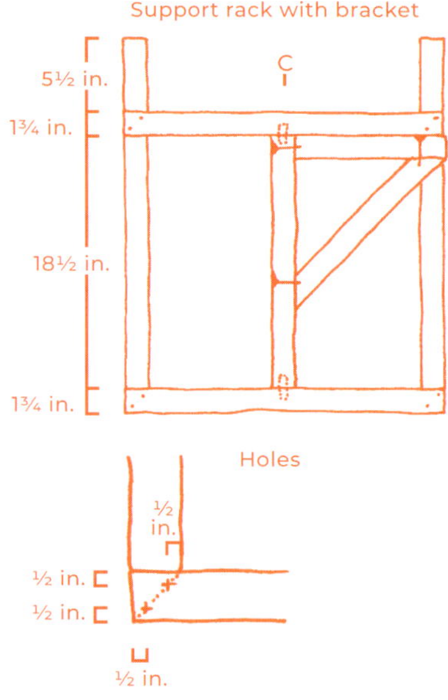

STEP 11 Sand the ends on all the pieces with 120-grit sandpaper and a sanding block. Then, sand all the pieces with 240-grit sandpaper; smooth the edges and corners.

STEP 12 Arrange all the pieces that will be joined on the work surface. Begin with the lowest part and bore with the 9⁄64-inch (3.5mm) bore down through the previously bored holes in the two vertical pieces. Apply glue to the contact surfaces and then firmly screw with the 5⁄32-by-1⅜-inch (4 × 35mm) brass or rustproof steel screws. Double check for a 90° angle with a try square.

STEP 13 Tap the wooden pegs into the holes on the bracket, without glue, and then set the bracket in place on the support rack, with the pegs down in the holes on the horizontal part of the support rack. Place the top horizontal piece on the support rack so the bracket is locked between them. Make sure the spacing between the two horizontal pieces is the same on both sides. The spacing should be 5⁄64 inches (2 mm) larger than the length of the bracket, so it can move between them. When all the pieces have been correctly placed, bore and glue the top piece exactly as for the lower one.

STEP 14 Screw the hinge on the end of the tabletop support. The hinge should sit with the joint downward, and the joint should be aligned with the lower edge of the end (see illustration on next page). Bore with a 3⁄32-inch (2.5mm) bore before you screw the hinge down firmly with a ⅛-by-¾-inch (3 × 20mm) brass screw.

STEP 15 Lay the hanging rack on the work surface and then lay the tabletop on top of it so it'll look like the table is folded down. Lay the tabletop so that the hinge is placed with the joint aligned with the under edge of the top slat (see drawing). Make sure that the tabletop lies edge to edge with the

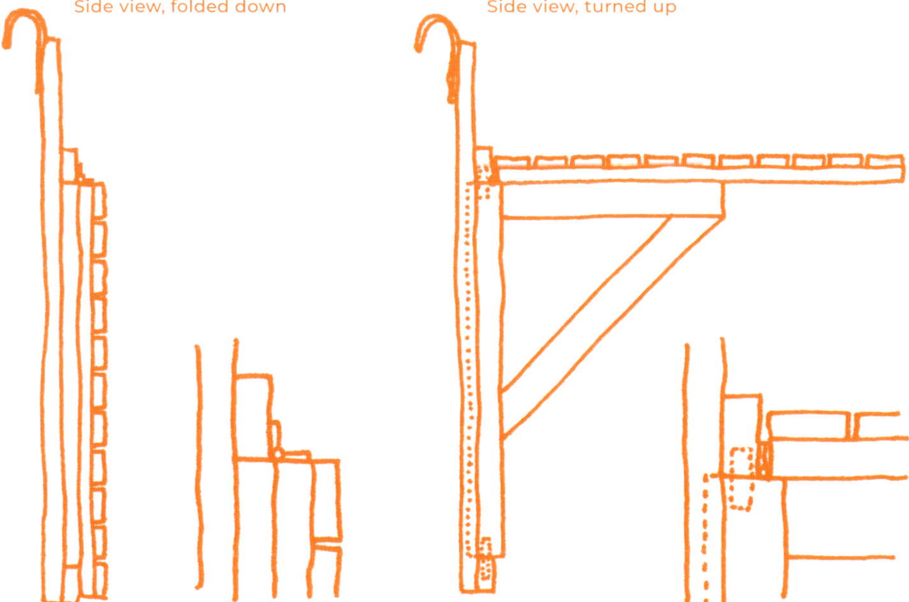

support rack. Pre-bore and then firmly screw the hinge to the support rack.

STEP 16 Oil the entire table with boiled linseed oil. Use a brush and let the oil soak in for about 20 minutes. Wipe off any excess oil. Repeat once the first application has dried.

STEP 17 Firmly screw in the hooks that you'll hang the table up with into the balcony. The height to hang it at depends on how high of a banister you have. The height of the tabletop should be about 29½ inches (750 mm) from the floor. Screw it down firmly with ⅛-by- ¾-inch (3 × 20mm) round-head screws.

PLANTER BOX WITH TRELLIS

Trellises are a great way to grow plants along a facade or for a protected area.

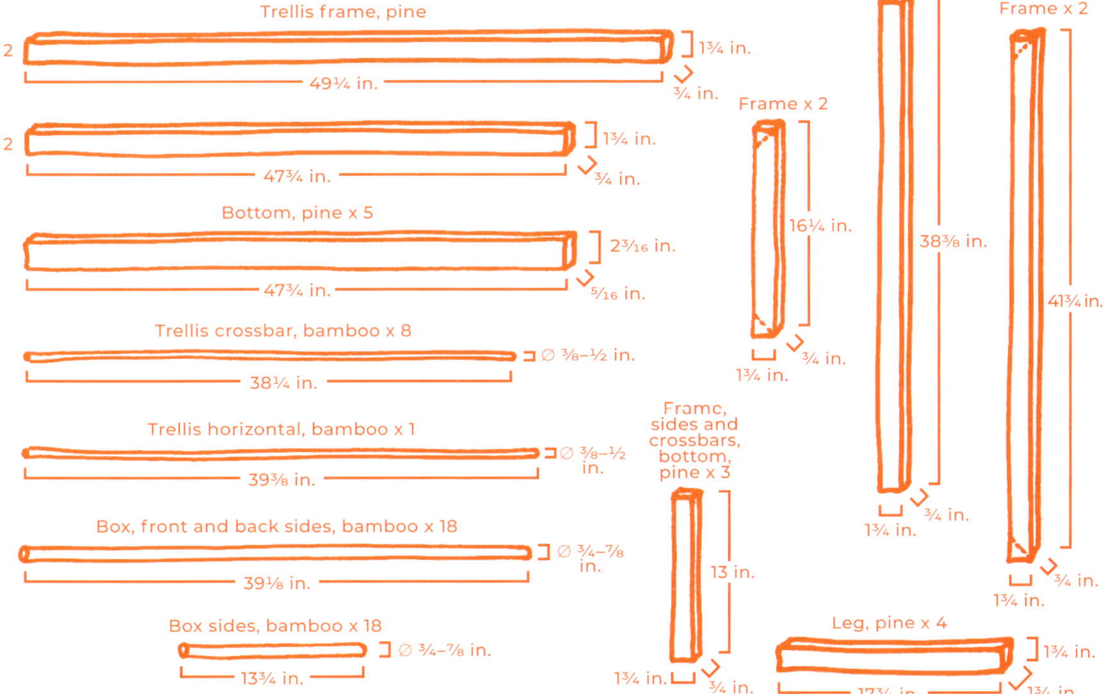

TOOLS

Japanese saw
Miter box
Try square
Auger bore
9⁄16 and ¾ inch (15 and 20 mm)
Sandpaper, 180
Sanding block
Bore ⅛ and 5⁄32 inch (3 and 4 mm)
Screwdriver and bits
Countersink
Rasp or carving knife
Rubber mallet

MATERIALS

18 x 39⅛ in. (26 m) bamboo rods, ¾–⅞ in. (20–22mm) in diameter
1 x 39⅜ in. and 8 x 38¼ in. (10 m) bamboo rods, ⅜–½ in. (10–12 mm) in diameter
4 x 17¾ in. (2.5 m) planed pine, 1¾ x 1¾ in. (43 x 43 mm)
3 x 13 in., 2 x 16¼ in., 2 x 38⅛ in., 2 x 41¾ in., 2 x 47¼ in., and 2 x 49¼ in. (12 m) planed pine, ¾ in. x 1¾ in. (21 × 43 mm)
5 x 47¾ in. (6 m) planed pine, 5⁄16 × 2 3⁄16 in. (8 × 56 mm)
16 wood screws, ⅛ × 1⅝ in. (3 × 42 mm)
20 rustproof screws, countersunk heads, 5⁄32 × 2¾ in. (4 × 70 mm)
12 rustproof screws, countersunk heads, 5⁄32 × 1⅜ in. (4 × 35 mm)
10 rustproof screws, countersunk heads, ⅛ × 1 in. (3 × 25 mm)
78¾ in. (2 m) hemp rope
Wood glue for exterior
Boiled linseed oil

STEP 1 Measure and cut all the materials to the specified length (see illustrations on previous page). Use the try square when drawing lines, and cut in the miter box with a Japanese saw. The pieces for the frame have 45° angles on both ends, so use a square with 45° on the handle or use a sliding T bevel. Then, cut the 45° angles in the miter box.

STEP 2 Sort the pieces into three different piles: legs, frame, and box. Begin with the legs.

Decide which legs will be at the front and back, right and left, and mark them so you can remember which is which; for example, LB (left back), RB (right back), LF (left front), and RF (right front). On each leg, also mark the place to bore for the bamboo rods (see measurements on drawing below). Now, bore the holes with a ¾-inch (20mm) auger bore. The holes should be 9⁄16 inch (14 mm) deep. It's important that the holes are not any deeper or more shallow.

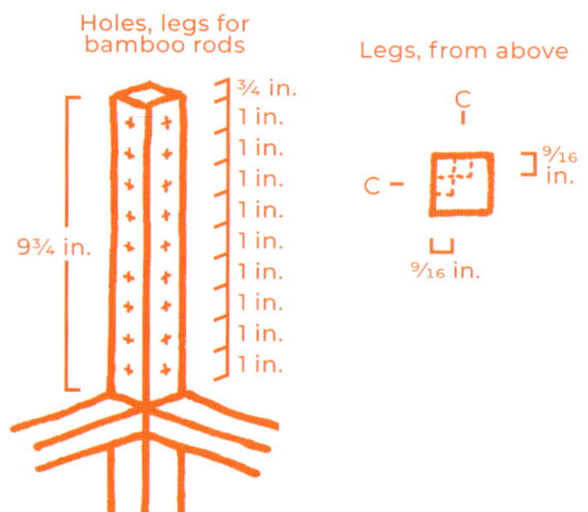

STEP 3 Pre-bore the legs with a 5⁄32-inch (4mm) bore where the frame pieces will be screwed in (see measurements on drawing below). Note that the holes sit diagonally on one side of the leg and horizontally on the other side. This is so that the holes won't intersect each other. Countersink the hole.

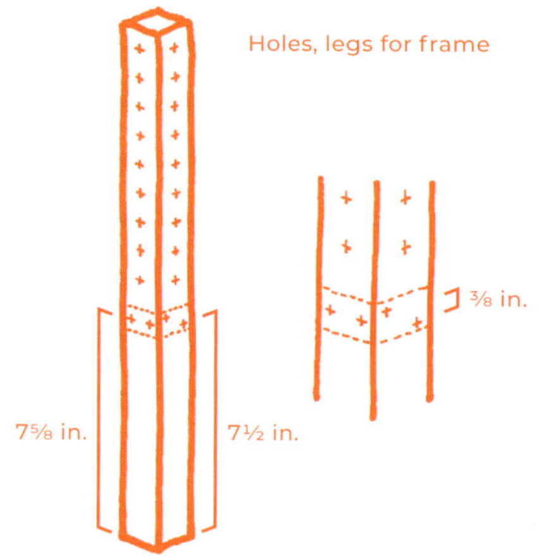

STEP 4 Sand the legs with 180-grit sandpaper and a sanding block; break edges and corners.

STEP 5 Make sure that each bamboo rod for the box goes into a ¾-inch (20mm) hole on a leg. If not, make adjustments with a carving knife or rasp until everything fits into each hole's depth.

STEP 6 When all the bamboo rods fit into the holes, it's time to join the box pieces with the legs. Double check to see that the saw cuts on the frame pieces are at 90°. If not, make adjustments with a rasp until everything fits.

STEP 7 Begin by assembling the short sides. First, glue and screw the frame on the short side on one of the legs with a 5⁄32-by-2¾-inch (4 × 70mm) screw (see measurements in the drawing on previous page). Then tap the bamboo rods into the holes on that leg. Now you can put the bamboo rods into the holes on the next leg. This might be a bit fiddly. If you can find an extra pair of hands, the task will be easier. Otherwise, you'll just need some extra patience. When you have the bamboo rods in the holes, you can pound them in with a rubber mallet so all of them go in well. Measure the distance between the legs at the topmost bamboo rod and make sure it's not more than the frame. If it's bigger, not all the bamboo rods will likely fit in properly. If the measurements match, you can screw and securely glue the frame and legs.

Do the same on the other short side.

STEP 8 Once both short sides have been joined, you can continue with the long sides. Begin by pre-boring the holes in the frame for the crossbars for the bottom (see measurements on drawing). Use a 5⁄32-inch (4mm) bore and countersink the holes. Then, work as you did for the short sides, although now you must make both the front side and back side at the same time. Glue and screw both frame pieces in the one short side and then insert the long bamboo rods into the holes on the legs. This will be easiest if you have the short sides lying on the floor. When the bamboo rods have been inserted, take the other short side and insert the bamboo rods, one after the other. This will be twice as fiddly as with the short sides, so be patient! When all the rods are in, hit them with a rubber mallet so they go down to the bottom. Check all the measurements. When they are all in properly, screw the frame pieces to the other short side.

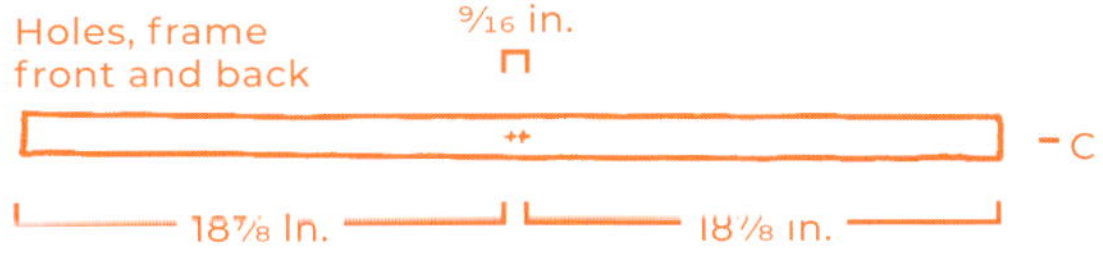

STEP 9 Stand the box on its feet and set the frame on it. Make sure that all the miters fit well together; otherwise make adjustments with a rasp. Sand and smooth the edges with 180-grit sandpaper and a sanding block.

STEP 10 Pre-bore the holes for the frame pieces with a ⅛-inch (3mm) bore and then glue and screw them firmly down in the legs on the box with the ⅛-by-1⅝-inch (3 × 42mm) wood screws.

STEP 11 Now continue with the bottom. First, firmly screw the crossbar to the frame pieces with the 5⁄32-by-2¾-inch (4 × 70mm) screws through the previously bored holes.

STEP 12 Pre-bore holes in the end and middle of the bottom slats, following the measurements on the drawing. Bore with a ⅛-inch (3mm) bore and countersink the holes. Then, sand and break the edges with 180-grit sandpaper and a sanding block.

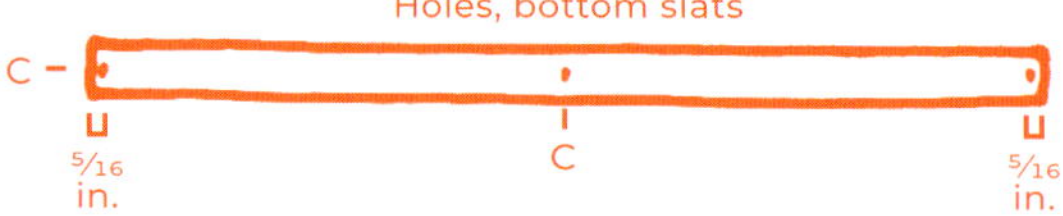

STEP 13 Firmly screw the bottom slats on the crossbar and frame pieces on the short sides with the ⅛-by-1-inch (3 × 25mm) screws, following the drawing below.

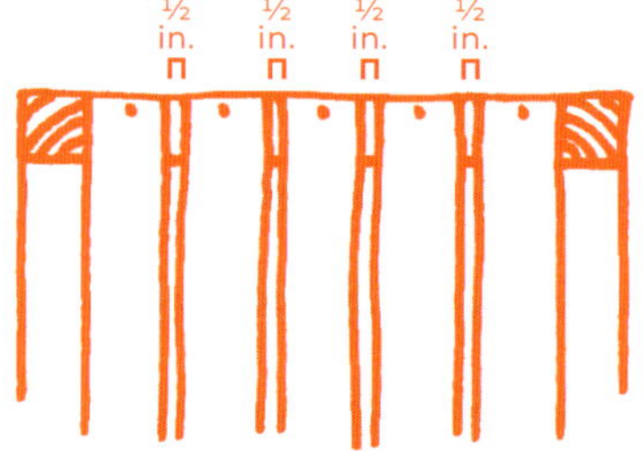

STEP 14 The planter box is now finished, and you can continue with the trellis: Pre-bore all the holes in the trellis frame (see measurements on drawing on next page). Bore the holes for the bamboo rods with a 9⁄16-inch (15mm) auger bore, 9⁄16 inch (15 mm) deep. Bore the holes for the joints with the box and the holes for joining the frame itself with a 5⁄32-inch (4mm) bore and countersink.

STEP 15 Sand and break the edges on the slats with 180-grit sandpaper and a sanding block. Screw and glue the frame together with the 5⁄32-by-1⅜-inch (4 × 35mm) screws through the previously bored holes. See illustration for placement of the slats. Make sure that the holes for the bamboo rods are turned inward.

STEP 16 Now you can ease the bamboo rods into the holes. Bamboo is quite flexible but also very hard, so you can

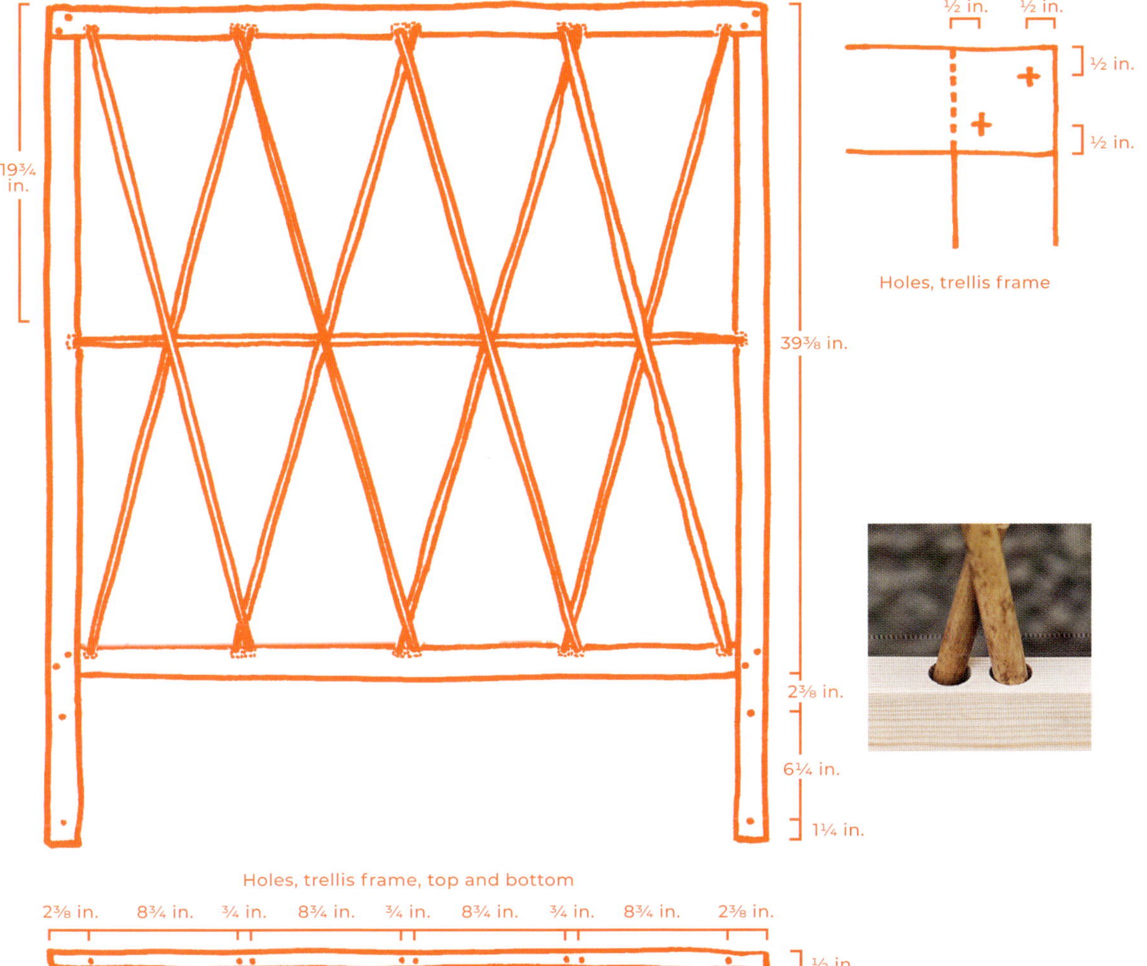

flex them a bit to insert them. First inset a rod into a hole and bend the rod a little in the middle so it'll go into the second hole. Begin with those leaning in the same direction, then take those leaning in the opposite direction. Finally, take the horizontal ones that will be in the middle of the frame. You set it so it's placed behind the crossed rods. You can see how the pattern looks in the drawing.

Now bind the bamboo rods together, with the hemp rope crisscrossing on the trellis.

STEP 17 Apply oil to the pine pieces with a brush. Let the wood absorb the linseed oil for about 20 minutes. Wipe off any excess oil. Once the first layer has dried, repeat the process. The bamboo does not need any finishing.

STEP 18 Place the pots with your chosen plants so they'll climb up the trellis. You can also staple canvas inside the box and plant directly in the box if you prefer.

PLANTING TABLE

A wheeled planting table can be moved around as you like. The nifty tabletop can be lifted so rainwater won't accumulate on it.

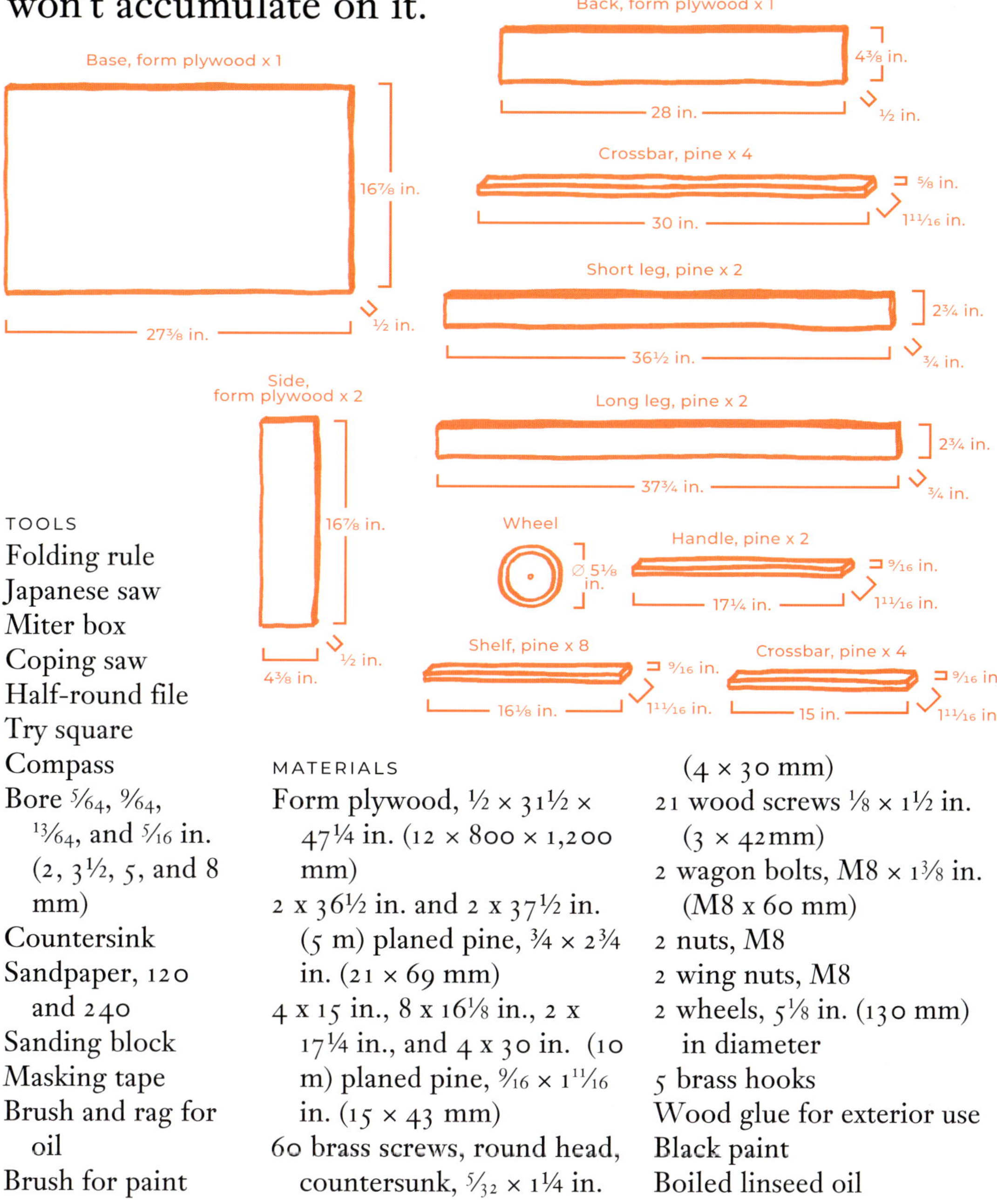

TOOLS

Folding rule
Japanese saw
Miter box
Coping saw
Half-round file
Try square
Compass
Bore 5/64, 9/64, 13/64, and 5/16 in. (2, 3½, 5, and 8 mm)
Countersink
Sandpaper, 120 and 240
Sanding block
Masking tape
Brush and rag for oil
Brush for paint

MATERIALS

Form plywood, ½ × 31½ × 47¼ in. (12 × 800 × 1,200 mm)
2 x 36½ in. and 2 x 37½ in. (5 m) planed pine, ¾ × 2¾ in. (21 × 69 mm)
4 x 15 in., 8 x 16⅛ in., 2 x 17¼ in., and 4 x 30 in. (10 m) planed pine, 9/16 × 1 11/16 in. (15 × 43 mm)
60 brass screws, round head, countersunk, 5/32 × 1¼ in. (4 × 30 mm)
21 wood screws ⅛ × 1½ in. (3 × 42mm)
2 wagon bolts, M8 × 1⅜ in. (M8 x 60 mm)
2 nuts, M8
2 wing nuts, M8
2 wheels, 5⅛ in. (130 mm) in diameter
5 brass hooks
Wood glue for exterior use
Black paint
Boiled linseed oil

STEP 1 Have the form plywood cut to specified dimensions at the lumberyard. See measurements on drawing on previous page.

STEP 2 Measure and cut the remaining materials for the legs, following the illustrations on previous page. Use a try square when marking and a Japanese saw and miter box for cutting.

STEP 3 Draw the rounding on one end of the legs, using a compass. Make sure that the half circle goes all the way out to the edges and end. Cut out the half circle with a coping saw. File to make the rounding nice and even. Then bore the holes in the center of the circle with a 5/16-inch (8mm) bore on the back leg (see drawing below).

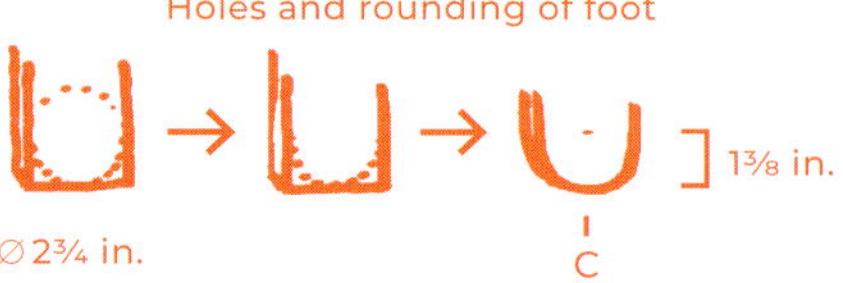

STEP 4 Pre-bore holes in the crossbars, handle, and shelf battens with a 13/64-inch (5mm) bore (see measurements on illustration). Then countersink the holes. Adjust the depth of the countersinking to the head on the brass screws.

STEP 5 Sand the ends on all the pieces with 120-grit sandpaper and a sanding block. Lightly sand all the pieces with 240-grit sandpaper and then break the edges.

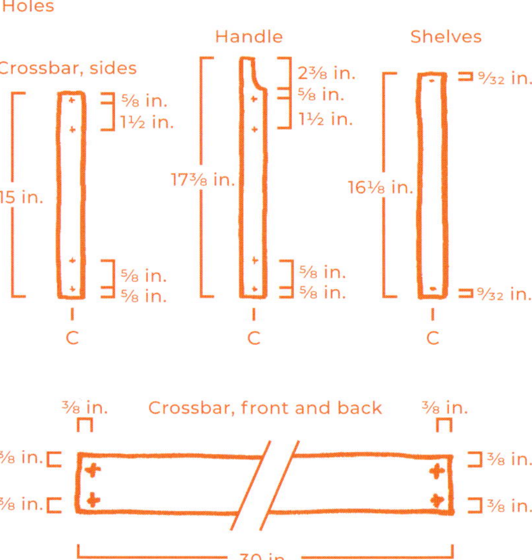

STEP 6 Set a pair of legs (a front and a back leg) on your work surface. As you can see, the legs are different lengths because the wheels sit on the back legs and will add more height. Measure from the top of the leg when you mark where the two side crossbars will be screwed in (see measurements on illustration).

STEP 7 Arrange the side crossbars. The ends of the crossbars should be aligned with the outer edge of the leg. Pre-bore with a 9/64-inch (3.5mm) bore through the previously bored holes in the crossbars on lower leg. Glue and screw in the 5/32-by-1¼-inch (4 × 30mm) screws. If you chose to use brass screws, you need to be careful when screwing them, in because brass is a soft metal that can break if you aren't careful. Do the same with the other pair of legs.

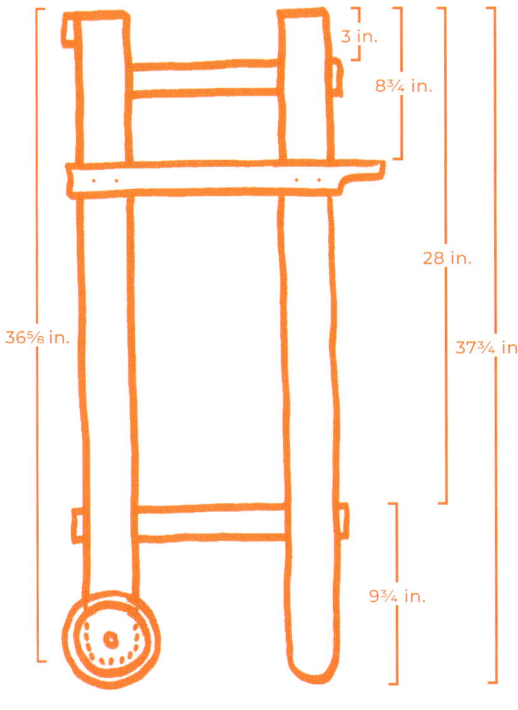

Leg setup, side view

STEP 8 Now you can screw together the two sides with the front and back crossbars. The two front crossbars will align with those on the sides. Note that the bars should be on the inside of the legs (see drawing). Of the two bars on the back, the top one should be edge to edge with the ends of the legs, and the lower one aligned with the bottommost bars. Do the same with the sidebars: set in place, bore through the pre-bored holes, glue, and then firmly screw in.

STEP 9 Draw and then cut the cutouts on the handles (see measurements on drawing). Cut with a coping saw and file the saw cuts until they are smoothed. Sand with 120-grit sandpaper and smooth the edges.

STEP 10 Measure and screw on handles on the sides (see measurements on drawing). Do the same with the crossbars.

STEP 11 Now only the pieces for the shelf are left to do before the assembly is finished. Glue and firmly screw in the pieces, following measurements on drawing. Do the same here as for the crossbars: pre-bore, glue, and screw with $\frac{5}{32}$-by-1¼-inch (4 × 30mm) screws.

Spacing of battens, shelf

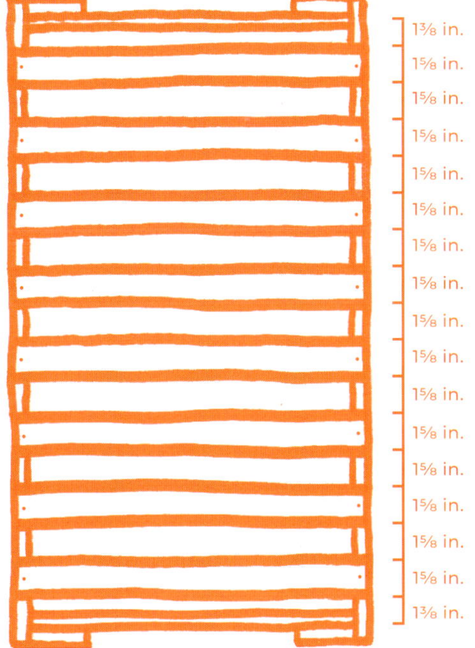

STEP 12 Use a brush to apply oil to the leg assembly. Let the wood absorb the oil for about 20 minutes, and then wipe off any excess oil with a rag. Repeat once the first application has dried.

STEP 13 Pre-bore holes in the form plywood with a 5/64-inch (2mm) bore, following the measurements on the drawing below. Then, screw the pieces together with the 1/8-by-1½-inch (3 × 42mm) wood screws. First screw the bottom to the side walls and then the back. You do not need to glue before screwing. Wood glue does not adhere on form plywood.

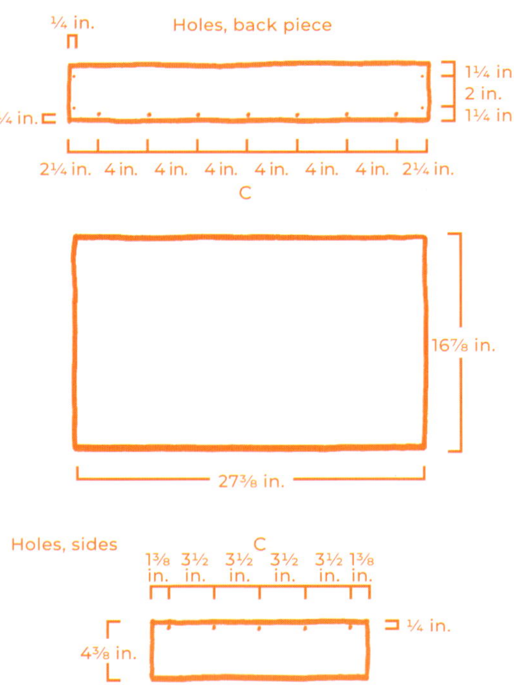

STEP 14 Sand the end wood with 240-grit sandpaper and a sanding block. Break edges. Now you can paint the end wood of the plywood if you want. If you prefer to keep the wood as is, you can apply boiled linseed oil on it instead.

Protect with masking tape wherever you think necessary. Once the paint/oil has dried, you can sand gently with 240-grit sandpaper and then apply one more layer of paint/oil.

STEP 15 Attach the wheels to the legs, using bolts as wheel axles. Screw in a nut and a wingnut on each bolt and screw in both so they fit in about 1/32 inch (1 mm) from the wood so the wheels can turn. Then tension the nuts and wingnuts hard against each other to allow them to lock.

STEP 16 Bore a hole with the 5/64-inch (2mm) bore into the bottom edge of the front crossbar for the hooks if you want them (see measurements on drawing below). Screw the hooks in, using a pen or chisel as a lever.

Now, all you have to do is begin planting!

Holes, front crossbar

3⅛ in. 6 in. 6 in. C 6 in. 6 in. 3⅛ in.

STORAGE BENCH

Where will you put all those hooks, cushions, and pegs that you use outside on the balcony? Of course, you just need to make a storage bench! This one has a loose lid and webbing for the bottom, a little trick so a bunch of stuff won't collect on the bottom.

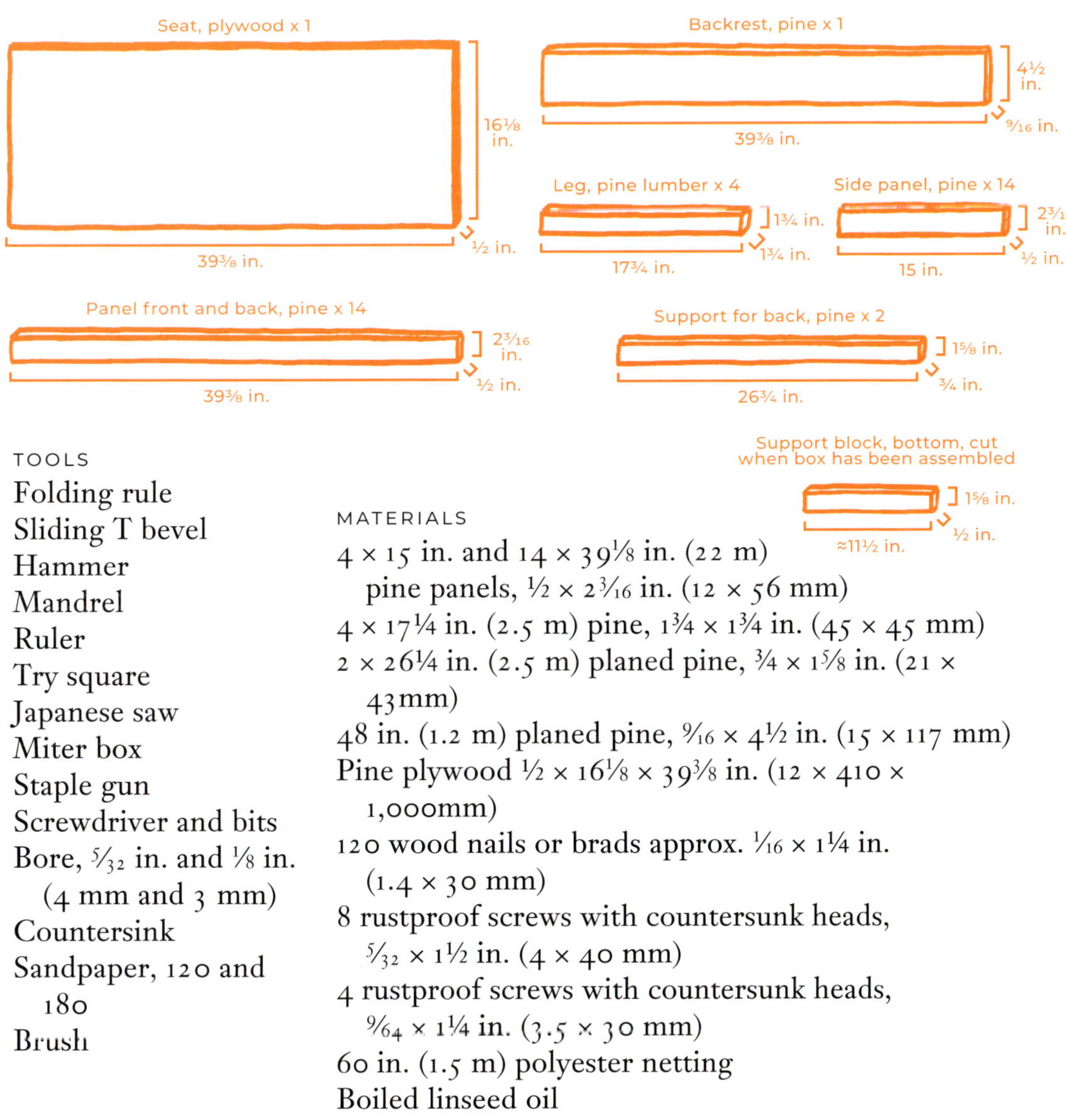

TOOLS

Folding rule
Sliding T bevel
Hammer
Mandrel
Ruler
Try square
Japanese saw
Miter box
Staple gun
Screwdriver and bits
Bore, ⁵⁄₃₂ in. and ⅛ in. (4 mm and 3 mm)
Countersink
Sandpaper, 120 and 180
Brush

MATERIALS

4 × 15 in. and 14 × 39⅛ in. (22 m) pine panels, ½ × 2³⁄₁₆ in. (12 × 56 mm)
4 × 17¼ in. (2.5 m) pine, 1¾ × 1¾ in. (45 × 45 mm)
2 × 26¼ in. (2.5 m) planed pine, ¾ × 1⅝ in. (21 × 43mm)
48 in. (1.2 m) planed pine, ⁹⁄₁₆ × 4½ in. (15 × 117 mm)
Pine plywood ½ × 16⅛ × 39⅜ in. (12 × 410 × 1,000mm)
120 wood nails or brads approx. ¹⁄₁₆ × 1¼ in. (1.4 × 30 mm)
8 rustproof screws with countersunk heads, ⁵⁄₃₂ × 1½ in. (4 × 40 mm)
4 rustproof screws with countersunk heads, ⁹⁄₆₄ × 1¼ in. (3.5 × 30 mm)
60 in. (1.5 m) polyester netting
Boiled linseed oil

STEP 1 Have the plywood cut to the specified measurements at the lumberyard. To make your bench look nicer, I recommend that you buy better-quality plywood, but you could also use regular builder's plywood.

STEP 2 Cut the panels, following the measurements in the illustration on the previous page. Use a try square when drawing the lines, and cut with a Japanese saw and miter box.

STEP 3 Lay out the seven pieces that will form the panel on the front as they will be placed for assembly. Make sure that they all lie edge to edge at a 90° angle. Number the pieces 1–7 so you can easily see the order in which they'll be placed. Make a mark 1¼ inches (30 mm) in from both ends on the top piece. The mark should be made on the top edge of the piece. Then, draw a straight line from the mark to the corner of the lowest piece's lower edge. Use a ruler or something similar so the line will be completely straight from the mark to the corner (see illustration below). Cut each piece, following the line you drew.

Do the same thing with the seven pieces for the back panel.

STEP 4 Now you can cut the legs, but before you do, you'll need to prepare the angles you'll cut at. Place the sliding T bevel against the saw cuts on one of the pieces you cut in step 3, so the bevel copies this angle. Lock the bevel and transfer the angle to the leg, at both top and bottom (see measurements on illustration). The angle is about 5°. Because it can be a little tricky to cut at an angle, it would be easier if you draw a line to cut on all four sides. The front side and backside should be at an angle, and the inside and outsides should be at 90°. Begin by cutting one leg freehand (see page 25), but when you cut the other three legs, you can use the first leg as a sawing block (see page 25).

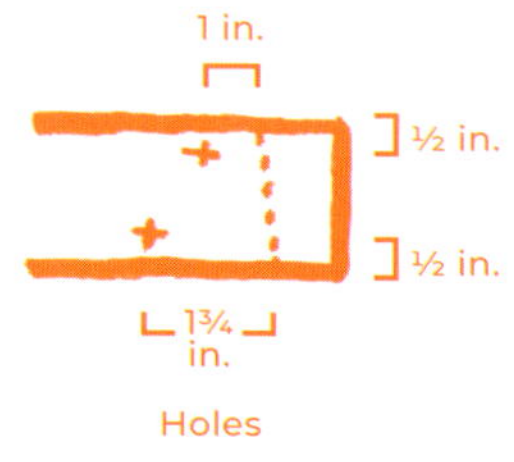

STEP 5 Mark the places for nailing on the pieces (see drawing). Tap the nails in only partially on the pieces so they just sit in place.

STEP 6 Lay out all seven pieces for the front panel on two of the legs in the order that they will be nailed. Because the pieces on the front will cover the sidepieces, they will stick out ½ inch (12 mm) from the edge of the leg on both sides. The simplest way to make sure that they are correctly spaced is to use a ½-inch (12mm) piece of panel as a template. Lay the pieces very close to each other, with the top one edge to edge with the top end of the leg. Nail the top and bottom pieces first and then nail the remaining ones in between. Always double check the overhang with the little panel piece before you completely nail the pieces, and make sure that they are well aligned with each other. Make the backside the same way.

STEP 7 Now you can nail the pieces for the short side panels. The sidepieces should be aligned with those from the front and back. First nail the pieces of one side to those on the front, and then the other side's pieces to those on the back, so you have two L-shaped pieces. The easiest way to do this is if you have an area where the legs and panels to be nailed can rest, but, because a table is too low, you can, for example, place a pile of books high enough so the front/back can come up from the mark. That way, you'll have the advantage of a blunt surface to nail against.

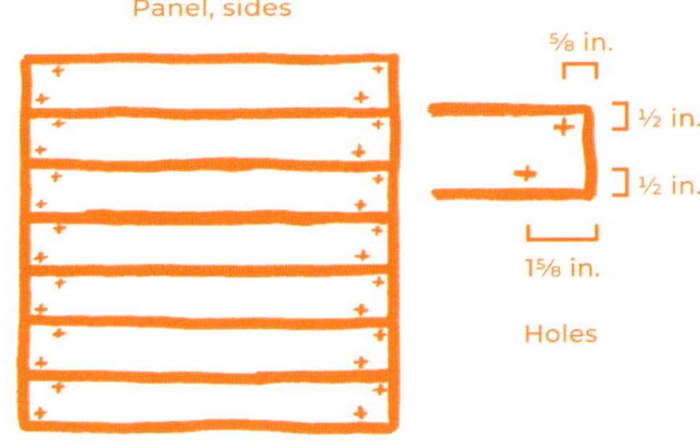

STEP 8 Arrange the L-shaped pieces as a box and nail them firmly to each other. Begin with one short side and then do the other. You could also begin with the top and bottom pieces so you lock in the shape, and then you can nail the rest. When all the nails have been hammered in, you can reinforce them by going over each with a mandrel (see page 44).

STEP 9 For the lid to lie in place, you should screw on two stop blocks. Lay the lid up and down on the plywood. The plywood should lie so that what will be the top side is turned down to the floor or work surface. Lay them edge to edge and make sure that you have 1¼ inches (30 mm) sticking out on both short sides. Use a pencil to mark inside the box along the short sides and legs. Remove the box and measure how long the spacing is between the front and back legs, using your markings. Cut two pieces of 1⅝-by-¾-inch (43 × 21mm) planed pine, slightly shorter (a few millimeters) than your measurements at the front. Use the miter box. Pre-bore with the 5⁄32-inch (4mm) bore countersink, glue, and then securely screw the two pieces with the 9⁄64-by-1¼-inch (3.5 × 30mm) screws precisely inside the drawn markings.

STEP 10 Staple the fabric inside the box. Staple it on the second piece from below and make sure that the net is quite taut.

STEP 11 Cut the pieces for the backrest to the specified length (see measurements in the drawing on page 165). Use the try square and draw the lines and then cut, using a Japanese saw and miter box.

STEP 12 Sand the corners of the box until they feel nice, and smooth any sharp edges. Use 120-grit sandpaper and a sanding block. Avoid sanding the pieces if they don't need it, because they already have a fine planed surface. Sand the plywood sheet with 180-grit sandpaper and break the edges and corners. Also break the edges and sand the ends on the pieces of the backrest.

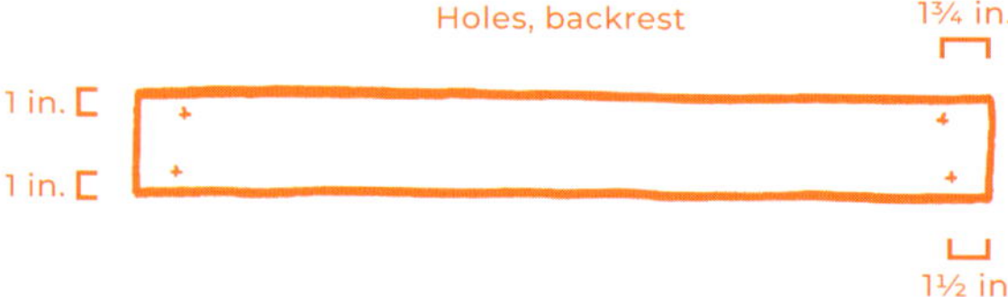

STEP 13 Bore the holes in the pieces for the backrest, following the illustration below. Use the 5⁄32-inch (4mm) bore and then countersink the holes.

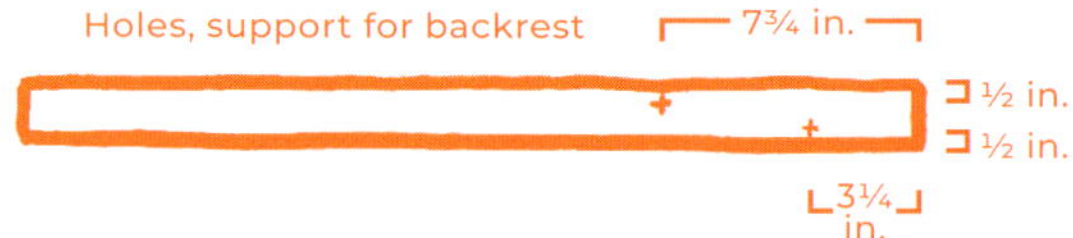

STEP 14 Mark on the box where the supports for the backrest will be screwed in (see illustration). Now place one support where it'll sit, and pre-bore with a ⅛-inch (3mm) bore into the box through your previously bored hole. Do likewise on the other side.

STEP 15 Screw on the two side supports with the 5⁄32-by-1½-inch (4 × 40mm) screws.

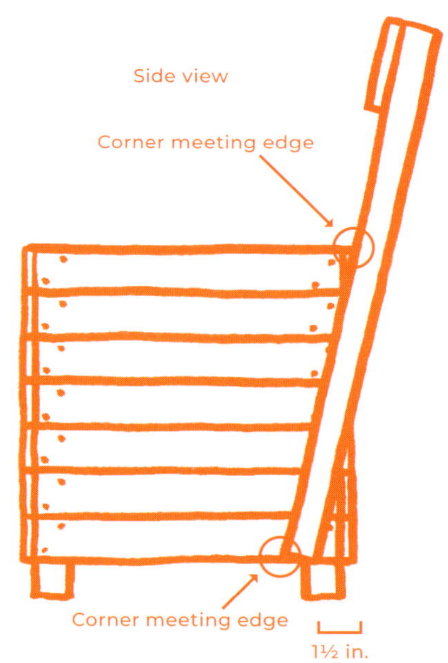

STEP 16 Do the same with the backrest plank, hold it in place, pre-bore, and then screw in firmly. To make it easier, you can set a clamp on one side to hold the pieces in place when you screw in the other; otherwise, you can screw in the top two screws first and then the two lower ones.

STEP 17 Apply boiled linseed oil with a brush to the outside of the bench and let the wood absorb the oil for 20 minutes. Wipe off any excess oil. Once the first application has dried, do another one.

STACKED GARDENING BOXES

Those of us with a balcony know that it can be difficult to find room for all the herbs, flowers, and vegetables we want to grow—for that reason, I like this arrangement with three planter boxes stacked up. I recommend that you measure your own balcony or outdoor space and adjust my measurements, so you'll have an arrangement that suits you perfectly!

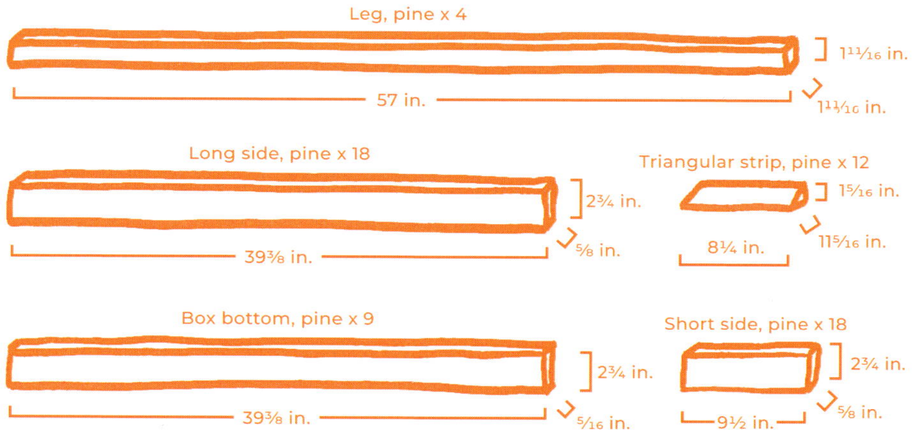

TOOLS

Folding rule
Japanese saw
Miter box
Screwdriver with bits
Wood bore ⅛, ⁵⁄₃₂, and ¹³⁄₆₄ in. (3, 4, and 5 mm)
Countersink
Try square
Sandpaper, 180
Sanding block
Staple gun
Brush and rag

MATERIALS

27 × 39⅜ in. (24 m) planed pine, ⁹⁄₁₆ × 2¾ in. (15 × 69 mm)
18 × 9½ in. (10 m) planed pine, ⁵⁄₁₆ × 2¾ in. (8 x 69mm)
12 × 8¼ in. (3 m) triangular strip in. pine, 1⁵⁄₁₆ x 1⁵⁄₁₆ in. (33 x 33 mm)
4 × 57 in. planed pine, 1¹⁄₁₆ × 1¹¹⁄₁₆ in. (27 × 43 mm)
110 rustproof screws with countersunk heads, ⁹⁄₆₄ × 1 in. (3.5 × 25 mm)
24 rustproof screws with round heads, ¹³⁄₆₄ × 2 in. (5 × 50 mm)
Wood glue for exterior use
Fabric for covering
Boiled linseed oil

STEP 1 Measure and cut the materials, following the drawings on the previous page. Mark wood, using a try square. Use a miter box and Japanese saw so that you can make straight cuts.

STEP 2 Divide the boards for the three boxes into three piles (six long sides, six short sides, three box bottoms, and four triangular strips in each pile). Bore holes in the box sides with the ⅛-inch (3mm) bore, following the illustration below. Note that there is only one hole in each end on the short sides and two holes in each end on the long sides. This is so the screws won't hit each other when the box is screwed together. Also, bore the holes in the bottom pieces with the ⅛-inch (3mm) bore and in the legs with the 13⁄64-inch (5mm) bore, following the drawing on the next page. Countersink the holes in the box sides and bottom pieces (see technique on page 37). The holes in the legs should not be countersunk.

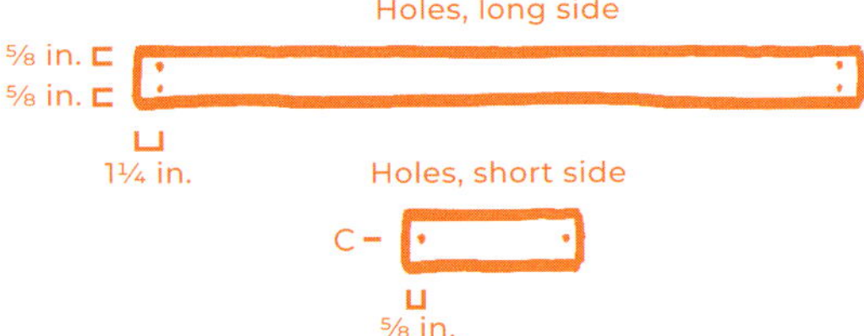

STEP 3 Begin by joining one of the short sides to one of the boxes. Start with the top board, apply a bit of glue, and lay it highest up on a triangular strip at a 90° angle. It should lie edge to edge at both end and side. When it's well-arranged, you can bore down a bit into the triangular strip with a ⅛-inch (3mm) bore, through the pre-bored hole in the short side. You work this way to prevent the triangular strip from splitting. Next, screw another triangular strip on the other end of the board the same way. Repeat the whole procedure with the short side board that will be bottommost. Lay it edge-to-edge with the triangular strip, glue, bore, and screw. Center the third board in between the top and bottom so there will be two equal-size gaps. The space in between is there so the wood can move, which can be necessary because the boxes might become too exposed to moisture. Repeat with all the remaining short sides.

STEP 4 Now work the same way with the long sides as you did for the short sides although you'll lay the board edge-to-edge with the sidepiece instead of the triangular strip. Glue, bore, and screw into the pre-bored hole precisely as above. Repeat with the remaining long sides.

STEP 5 Now it's time to glue and screw on the bottom boards. Begin with the two outermost panels and lay them edge to edge with the box. Firmly screw in the ⅛-by-¾-inch (3 × 20mm) screws. In this case, you don't need to pre-bore down into the box sides before you screw. Then securely screw the center plank with about the same size gap on each side. Repeat with the remaining bottom boards.

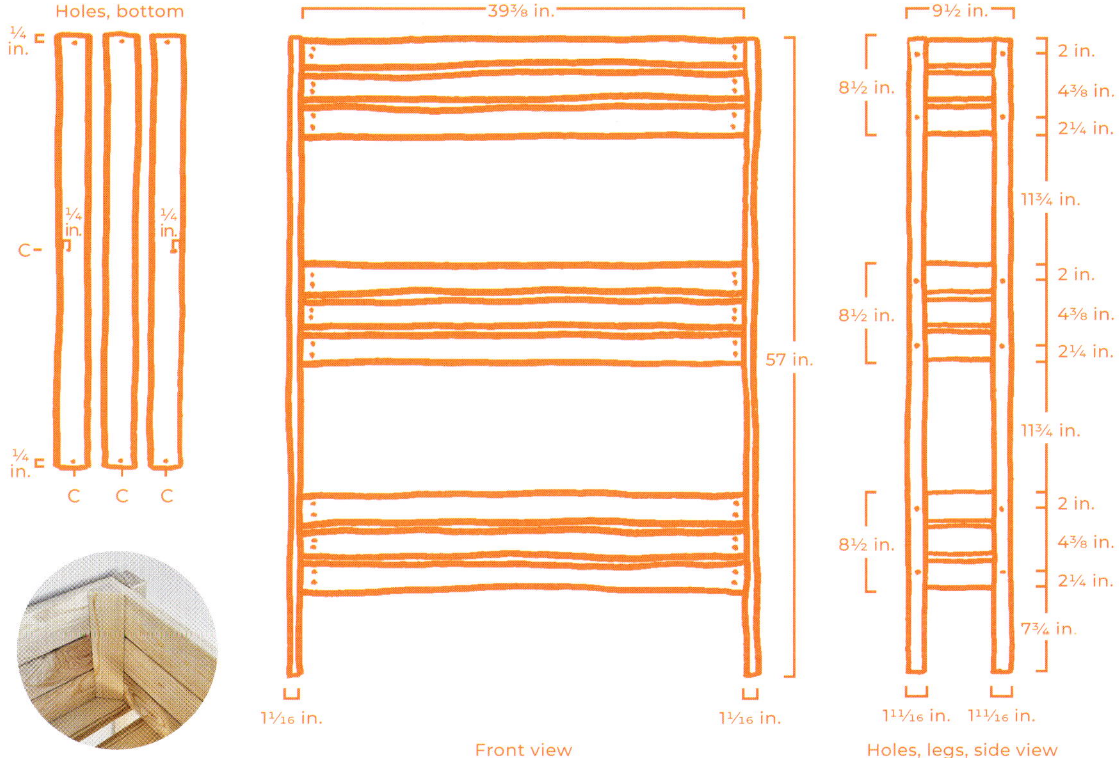

STEP 6 Cut the fabric to a size big enough for it to cover the inside of the boxes. Fold the corners in and staple the fabric in about ¾ inch (20 mm) from the top edge.

STEP 7 Smooth all the corners of the boxes and legs with 180-grit sandpaper.

STEP 8 Pre-bore holes in the legs with 13/64-inch (5mm) bore following the illustration above. Mark the places on the legs where the boxes will sit. Lay out the back legs and the three boxes on a flat surface with the backside downward, and then place all the pieces exactly as they will be joined. Apply glue to the contact surfaces and pre-bore through the holes with a 5/32-inch (4mm) bore and then screw the legs firmly onto the box with the 13/64-by-2-inch (5 × 50mm) screws. Turn the assembly and do the same thing with the front legs. Raise the planter boxes and make sure it stands steady on all four legs.

STEP 9 Use a brush to apply boiled linseed oil, and let the wood thoroughly absorb the oil. Wipe off any excess oil after about 20 minutes. Apply another layer of oil. When it's dry, you can begin planting!

CONVERSION TABLE (inches to millimeters)

1/8 in.	3 mm	4 13/16 in.	123 mm	17 3/8 in.	440 mm
5/32 in.	4 mm	5 in.	129 mm	17 3/4 in.	450 mm
13/64 in.	5 mm	5 1/8 in.	130 mm	18 1/8 in.	460 mm
1/4 in.	6 mm	5 1/2 in.	140 mm	18 1/2 in.	470 mm
9/32 in.	7 mm	6 in.	150 mm	18 9/16 in.	472 mm
5/16 in.	8 mm	6 1/8 in.	155 mm	18 7/8 in.	480 mm
3/8 in.	10 mm	6 1/4 in.	160 mm	19 3/4 in.	500 mm
1/2 in.	12 mm	7 in.	180 mm	20 1/4 in.	515 mm
9/16 in.	14 mm	7 1/4 in.	184 mm	20 5/8 in.	525 mm
5/8 in.	15 mm	7 1/2 in.	190 mm	20 7/8 in.	530 mm
1/3 in.	16 mm	7 3/4 in.	195 mm	23 5/8 in.	600 mm
3/4 in.	20 mm	7 7/8 in.	200 mm	26 5/8 in.	677 mm
7/8 in.	21.5 mm	8 1/4 in.	210 mm	26 3/4 in.	680 mm
1 in.	25 mm	8 3/4 in.	220 mm	27 3/16 in.	690 mm
1 1/16 in.	27 mm	9 1/2 in.	240 mm	27 1/2 in.	700 mm
1 3/16 in.	30 mm	9 5/8 in.	245 mm	28 in.	710 mm
1 3/8 in.	35 mm	10 1/4 in.	260 mm	28 3/4 in.	730 mm
1 1/2 in.	40 mm	11 in.	280 mm	29 1/2 in.	750 mm
1 3/4 in.	45 mm	11 1/2 in.	290 mm	30 in.	760 mm
1 7/8 in.	48 mm	11 3/4 in.	300 mm	31 in.	790 mm
2 in.	50 mm	12 3/16 in.	310 mm	31 1/2 in.	800 mm
2 3/16 in.	55 mm	12 5/8 in.	320 mm	34 5/8 in.	880 mm
2 3/8 in.	60 mm	12 15/16 in.	328 mm	35 1/2 in.	900 mm
2 9/16 in.	65 mm	13 in.	330 mm	36 1/4 in.	920 mm
2 3/4 in.	70 mm	13 3/8 in.	340 mm	37 3/4 in.	960 mm
2 7/8 in.	72 mm	13 3/4 in.	350 mm	38 1/4 in.	970 mm
3 in.	75 mm	14 in.	356 mm	38 3/8 in.	974 mm
3 1/8 in.	80 mm	14 1/4 in.	360 mm	39 1/8 in.	995 mm
3 3/8 in.	85 mm	15 in.	380 mm	39 3/8 in.	1000 mm
3 3/8 in.	86 mm	15 1/2 in.	395 mm	41 in.	1046 mm
3 1/2 in.	90 mm	15 3/4 in.	400 mm	41 3/4 in.	1060 mm
3 3/4 in.	95 mm	16 in.	405 mm	43 1/4 in.	1100 mm
4 in.	100 mm	16 1/8 in.	410 mm	47 1/4 in.	1200 mm
4 1/8 in.	105 mm	16 1/4 in.	414 mm	49 1/4 in.	1250 mm
4 1/4 in.	110 mm	16 3/8 in.	416 mm	57 in.	1450 mm
4 7/16 in.	112 mm	16 1/2 in.	420 mm	63 in.	1600 mm
4 9/16 in.	116 mm	16 7/8 in.	428 mm	86 5/8 in.	2200 mm
4 3/4 in.	120 mm	17 in.	430 mm		

INDEX OF KEYWORDS

THANK YOU

Mamma, because you let me sit and carve on the kitchen floor and, in addition, for all your continual encouragement and support.

Stefan, because you wanted to do this with me and for your great patience.

Ida and pappa, because you're so proud of me.

Stina, the best home carpenter I have had the pleasure of learning from, for ideas, help, and commitment.

Henrik and Maria at Natur & Kultur, for trusting me to write this book. It was such luck that I didn't know what I let myself in for!

Miki, for all the fine photos and all the hours behind the camera.

Anders and Martin, for your help.

Joel, for your extremely ambitious drawings for the bird feeder.

Fredells Builders in Sickla, for all the materials you contributed.

The forest, for all the trees.